ESCAPE FROM COMMUNISM

A true story and commentary

Truly free people can never be enslaved

BY DUMITRU SANDRU

Chivileri Publishing

ISBN 978-0-9836695-2-4

www.sandru.com

This book is dedicated to the hundreds of millions of people in the world who have suffered or died because of the inhumane political system called communism.

All the names of persons in this book, other than those of political leaders and my family, have been changed to protect their privacy.

Acknowledgements

Many thanks to Jonathan Kompara, Mihai Dumitrescu, John Hlava, Larry Hlava, Armen Abrahamian, Sofia Lilliam, and Gabriella Deponte

TABLE OF CONTENTS

Book 1. My Story 5

1. A Country That Is a Concentration Camp 7

2. Romania under Communism 13

3. Life under Communism 21

4. Mind Control and the Police State 31

5. It Was the Music 37

6. How to Intimidate the Population 39

7. Thinking about Going West 45

8. The Revolt 53

9. Back to School 59

10. A Different Turn of Events 67

11. Bad News 71

12. The Train Journey 75

13. Second Day, Saturday 79

14. Third Day, Sunday 89

15. Fourth day, Monday 91

16. Ollie's Uncle 96

17. To Italy 98

18. Near the Italian Border 102

19. Life as a Refugee in Italy............................110

20. In Retrospect..120

21. America, America.....................................122

Book 2. Communism *134*

1. What Is Communism? 136

2. Capitalism 140

3. The Proletariat and the Communist Revolution........144

4. Communism's Consolidation of Power 146

5. Nationalization 150

6. Killing the Opposition 154

7. Is Communism That Bad?............................160

8. How a Rich Country Becomes Poor under Communism 166

9. The Standard of Living Goes Down 172

10. Why Communism Is Doomed to Fail 180

Book 3. The United States of America.....................*186*

1. Politicians and Democracy 188

2. Entitlements 194

3. Taxes and Corporate Welfare.......................198

4. Wealth 200

5. The Future...204

BOOK 1. MY STORY

A True Story

I was born in 1953 in communist Romania, behind the Iron Curtain, and what an appropriate name that was. Life under communism was all I knew until I was eighteen, at which age I decided to risk my life and escape from the communist hell, also known as the "Proletariat's Paradise," that was then Romania. If you don't think getting out of a country is "escaping," you don't know what communism is, or how it works, or what it does to one's mind and soul. Risking my life to get across communist Romania's "Berlin Wall" was a better alternative than trying to survive under communism.

The following story is my true story, and I relate it here to the best of my recollection. I'm writing this story in 2012, forty-one years after it happened. I'm narrating this from the point of view I hold today, complemented by the information and knowledge I've acquired since then.

1. A COUNTRY THAT IS A CONCENTRATION CAMP

Most communist countries, and especially Romania in 1971, resemble concentration camps. If the Nazi concentration camps come to your mind, that's exactly what communist Romania was at the time, and it continued to be that until 1989, when communism finally came to an end in Romania and Central Europe.

A country of twenty million people, slightly smaller in size than the state of Oregon, was a concentration camp. All the country's borders – but especially its border with Yugoslavia – were dotted with sixty-foot-high watchtowers, electric and barbed wire fences, dikes, tripwires connected to tripflares for night illumination, mean dogs, and even meaner border patrols armed with Kalashnikovs. Perhaps it wasn't exactly the Berlin Wall, but this 1,600-mile-long fence all around Romania made the whole country into a virtual concentration camp. As a comparison, the border between the US and Mexico is 1,933 miles long, and, although some portions of the US-Mexico border have walls and fences, none of it comes close to resembling the Romanian border during communist times.

The Danube River makes up part of Romania's border, just like the Rio Grande forms part of the frontier between the US and Mexico. The Danube is the second-longest river in Europe; it can be as wide as a mile in certain sections, while in areas such as the Iron Gates, the narrows crossing the Carpathian Mountains, it can be constricted down to 800 feet, but the water is extremely treacherous there. Some people chose to cross into Yugoslavia across the Danube. It wasn't easy, even at night. The border patrols had high-speed boats with high-powered lights. Even on moonless nights, the river surface is reflective enough to expose any floating objects. Any swimmers or rafters could be easily seen, and the border patrols would scoop up the escapees from the water, sometimes even when they had already reached the Yugoslavian shore.

This heavily guarded border, by land or along the Danube River, was not to keep the illegal aliens or foreign invaders out – although that was the official reason – but to keep the country's people within its borders. In the case of the US, many foreigners want to come here legally or illegally, but in Romania many, if not most Romanians, wanted to *get out* legally or illegally. I wish I could have left Romania legally, but that was nearly impossible, so I chose the desperate and dangerous illegal way.

The border patrols were ordered to stop and arrest anyone who attempted a border crossing. And the guards were free to shoot escapees if they weren't able to capture them. I don't know what the consequences were for the border patrols that did not catch an escapee, but the reward for apprehending one was a week's furlough from military duty (the border patrol was part of the armed forces). A week off was a great incentive for the soldiers to keep the borders secured.

If a person was spotted attempting to get near the border, and that person was not permitted to be there, the border patrol would capture him or her. (Yes, there were gutsy or desperate women as well who tried to escape.) After they took you into custody, they wouldn't release you with just a warning: "Now go home and don't do this again." Arrest and incarceration were the inevitable punishment.

More often than not, the captured were severely beaten by the border patrols. After the patrols had had their "fun," the prisoners were taken to the police – or the militia, as it was known then – where they were interrogated. In communist Romania there was no such thing as having your Miranda Rights read, or getting one free phone call, or obtaining an attorney. An arrested individual was assumed guilty until proven innocent, which seldom happened.

The police kept the arrestees jailed for as long as they wished, or until they obtained a satisfactory confession out of them. The interrogation methods varied, depending on who the arrestees were, if they had attempted to escape in the past, if they looked suspicious, if they had prohibited items on them, or if they were associated with political dissidents. Most often than not, the interrogators administered another round of beatings if they suspected that the escapees had something to hide. Most of the people caught in their first attempt to escape lost their front teeth, and it wasn't from bad oral hygiene.

The brutal police interrogation was not meant to get the accused to admit their guilt, which was already proven since they were caught in the act, but to extract information about their political beliefs and whether they knew of others who might be inclined to attempt a similar escape. Under torture you would name your mother as a co-conspirator just to stop the pain.

The ultimate means of intimidating the population at large was fear. After such a traumatic experience, you would tell your friends what had happened. And your friends would tell their friends. Knowing the risk associated with seeking freedom, many would think twice before attempting to escape. People just bowed their heads and continued living a hopeless, desperate existence. Life under communism was hard: life expectancy was only sixty-six years, and many families had only one child, unwilling to bring more souls into that dismal world.

After a detainee confessed all his "crimes," he was sentenced and sent to prison. If he was lucky, and it was his first attempt, he got one year of hard labor. In communist jails, prisoners had to work; no TV or library for them. Their only exercise was hard work without pay. The not-so-lucky ones could spend up to five years in prison. One to five years of punishment just for wanting to be free!

An anecdotal figure I heard was that, of some 10,000 people who tried to cross the border illegally each year during those times, only 600 made it to Italy or Austria, the nearest free countries. Not all people trying to escape were caught at the Romanian border. Unfortunately for the Romanians, Romania was surrounded by other communist countries. Therefore, the task of reaching freedom was twice as hard; one had to get across another communist nation, Yugoslavia, and from that country cross its border illegally to the freedom of Italy or Austria.

Fortunately, Yugoslavia had a benign form of communism and was not as paranoid about keeping its population behind its borders, as was Romania. By the way, Romania was not alone in its border enforcement: Hungary, Poland, Bulgaria, Czechoslovakia, Albania, and – definitely – East Germany were as diligent in keeping their populations captive.

Nonetheless, Yugoslavia was not friendly toward the escapees from Romania, or Bulgaria, or Hungary, or the others. When the Yugoslavian police caught any of them, they were returned back to their respective countries. I heard that Romania paid in tons of salt for each person caught and returned (salt is abundant in Romania.)

From the Romanian border across Yugoslavia to Italy the distance is about 400 miles. This is the distance one had to traverse in a foreign country to reach freedom. Because the Yugoslavians didn't speak Romanian, if you made it across the border, you had to manage by sign language. The Romanian currency was worthless outside the country; you could not exchange it and buy a train ticket, for example. So most escapees had to walk, or, if they were lucky, they could hitchhike the distance. None of this was easy if you didn't speak the language, have any money, or know the territory. A Romanian escapee was easy pickings for the Yugoslavian police.

2. ROMANIA UNDER COMMUNISM

I was born and lived in Timisoara, a western city in the region of Banat, in the greater Transylvania area. Timisoara is the city where the Romanian anti-communist revolution started in 1989.

Opera House, Timisoara, Romania

View of the Cathedral, Timisoara, Romania

Romania had been communist since 1947, thanks to Stalin and his Soviet troops occupying the country. Communist operatives had rigged the elections, and a dark period descended over the country. Romania, along with Bulgaria, Hungary, Poland, Czechoslovakia, Albania, and East Germany, were the spoils of war the Soviet Union received for fighting against Nazi Germany. This voracious empire swallowed the whole of Central Europe. Unlike the Marshall Plan – instituted by the United States to rebuild West Germany – the Soviet Union instituted the Pillage, Rob, and Steal Plan to take everything of value from the occupied countries. Romania was rich in natural resources, and it was a fat cow to be milked, that is, until it began to show its horns.

I was too young to remember the years of hunger and turmoil after the war. My parents made sure that I did not go hungry or feel cold. For a kid not knowing any different, life was good. I was fed, I had a roof over my head, and I even had my own room. Medicine was socialized and free, and school was free, although that would not have been my concern at that age. My life was without any major pain, the way it should be for a kid.

That all changed once I hit puberty. From being a happy, blissfully ignorant child, I slowly became aware of the real world around me. My parents did not raise me to hate communism, because it would have been suicidal had they done so – a kid talks, and the authorities find out and imprison the mom and dad. My parents were not members of the communist party, and they had no sympathy for the regime in power. They talked to each other or their close circle of friends about the past, the realities of the present, and the future that seemed hopeless. I was to keep quiet about anything I overheard, which I did.

I learned that my mother's family was well-to-do before the communists took over. "Well-to-do" did not mean much to me then, since I had no point of reference about how life was like for a well-to-do family in a free, capitalist Romania. I found out that my mother's family did not inherit their fortune; they had worked their butts off to prosper, going from being a poor family to becoming business proprietors and landowners. My maternal grandfather, through hard work, frugality, and savings, managed before World War II to acquire a wheat flourmill, a sunflower oil production factory, hundreds of acres of wheat and corn and vineyards, and thousands of sheep. During one summer vacation when I was a kid, my cousin and I found hundreds of old, pre-communist Romanian coins hidden in the attic of my maternal grandmother's house. They were worthless then, but when my grandfather stashed them away for a rainy day, they had had substantial value.

After the communists took over the country, all private industry, banking, commerce, commercial real estate, and farmland were nationalized. Nationalization is a polite word for the robbery of private property by the state. Overnight, my mother's family had all its possessions confiscated by the government in the name of the people. Thirty years of hard work, sweat, and tears were gone in an instant. To add insult to injury, my mother's family were declared "exploiters of the people" – not wealth or job creators, but outright parasites. During those times, "exploiters of the people" were rounded up in the middle of the night and deported to labor camps in southeastern Romania, where most of them died. In a very short time, the hardest working and smartest section of the population was obliterated. It did not seem fair to me, even at that young age. My mother's family was lucky. They were not deported.

My grandfather died of a heart attack soon after the nationalization. My mother's family was allowed to keep their home and continued living there. Their land and the land of other private owners was confiscated as well and placed in collectives. A collective is a large farm that combines all the different parcels of land in an area. In theory, all the agricultural laborers own it, but the state is the custodian. In a collective, all members, regardless of whether they were landowners or not before the nationalization, become agricultural laborers.

My father's family came from a village in the mountainous region of Banat. They owned some land that, being hilly, could serve solely as a source of hay for livestock and as apple and plum orchards. My paternal grandfather, who I knew, was a master hooper, also known as a cooper. A hooper isn't someone who shoots hoops in basketball, but a craftsman who makes wood barrels and casks. Metal hoops hold the wooden slats in barrels together, so that's how the occupation got its name.

Since the land my father's family and others like them owned was made up of small parcels spread over many hills, it was difficult for the government to place them in collectives. Because they did not tip the scale to become "exploiters of the people," those landowners got to keep their land.

However, the communist idiocy affected my father. After my father was recruited into the military, he was selected to become an officer because he was an educated man. In officer's school, an eager-beaver lieutenant had the brilliant idea of collectivizing all the personal possessions in each dormitory. How would you like to be in a common dormitory with two dozen other young men, and share your comb, soap, brush and shaver, and toothbrush? Personal grooming objects were required to become available for common use. My father, just like any other self-respecting person, refused to share his toothbrush and other personal items with anyone.

As a consequence for disobeying orders, he was demoted to the rank of private and sent to a military labor camp. But it did not stop there: He was charged with subversion, and a political investigation was initiated against him and his family, accusing them of anti-communist activities and of being from "unhealthy roots," meaning a prosperous family, which was not true. The authorities couldn't make a case against him and discharged the investigation. Also, for the better, my father was stripped of his communist party membership. He had joined the party after the war, looking for "hope and change." Instead, Romanians got hopelessness and a miserable forty-two years of change.

If my father had been found guilty of any anti-communist sentiments, he could have been imprisoned at best, or shot at worst. My dad had heard enough horror stories about the atrocities committed by the communists against the politically incarcerated that he was ready to commit suicide rather than go to prison. Later, he found out from friends and acquaintances about the pressure put on them by the secret police to testify that he was a subversive. They refused. There were still men of honor out there.

The communist propaganda told us how lucky we all were to live in such good times, and how horrible and miserable life was under capitalism. But my parents, relatives, and their friends were telling a different story. Although Romania was behind the Iron Curtain, goods and information from the West leaked in, and the West did not seem to be so deplorable. Occasional movies from the West showing modern life played in movie theaters, and I was able to get a glimpse of what life was like on the other side of the Iron Curtain. Using a film analogy, the difference between communist Romania and the West was like watching a black and white movie with scratchy sound on a small screen versus watching a color movie with stereo sound on a panoramic screen.

I was young, but I was not a fool. It was not the fact that life in the West was better or more prosperous that irked me, but the fact that the communist government was lying to us. Once a government loses the trust of its people, everything the state says after that, even if it's true, has no value. As I know now, all governments lie. But at least there is freedom in the US to call out their lies. There was no such freedom under communism. And it wasn't only that you could not call out their lies, but you also had to believe the lies as truths. And if anyone questioned the communist truth, it was a capital offense against the communist party and the state.

As I was growing up, from time to time, I would hear about people who were arrested in the middle of the night for their political opinions. Their whereabouts afterward were unknown. If they were lucky, a few years later they would be released from prison, but they never seemed to be the same people as before. They spoke in soft voices or stared at the ground. My parents,

18

like many other people I knew, were horrified that they may be the next victims. As a matter of fact, they knew who the informants were at their workplaces or in the neighborhood, and kept a courteous distance from them. Those bastards could have ruined anyone's life, if they chose to do so.

However, such arrests in Romania were not made on a scale that rivaled what Stalin did in the Soviet Union. Only once in a while, if an enraged citizen let the truth out, an example had to be made of him to establish fear in the souls of the population. It worked every time. Fear works like magic, and the communists were masters of its use.

3. LIFE UNDER COMMUNISM

Life went on, bleak as it was: Go to school, joke and play with friends, chase girls, and occasionally see a good movie from the West, which provided a peephole through the Iron Curtain. We watched communist propaganda on TV, reminding us how prosperous we were, how heroic the communists had been in the sacrifices they had made to bring us communism and rescue us from capitalism. Romania's five-year plan was exceeded again, and our lives were getting better. And, of course, we were constantly told to economize. It was our patriotic duty.

Many times I stood in lines around the block for hours to buy meat or other hard-to-find items, which was just about everything. The basic staples in Romania were bread, potatoes, cooking oil, vegetables and fruits when they were in season, milk, cheese (one kind only), butter, eggs, sugar, and salt. However, if you did not buy some of these items early in the morning, you were bound to find the shelves empty by 5 p.m. The long lines were indisputable proof that Romania's five-year plan was being exceeded again and that our lives were getting better. Not.

Obviously, the professional party members, especially the ones in political and executive positions, did not have to wait in line like the rest of us in the proletariat. They had their own private stores, abundant with all the necessities. For some reason that I've since forgotten, I once ended up at the communist party headquarters, in the lunchroom reserved for party members only. They got free lunches and could take food home for dinner as well. By Romanian standards, that place looked like Christmas dinner, with a variety and abundance of dishes available for party members only. No starving for them.

Whenever a line formed in front of a store, people joined in, sometimes not knowing what would be available for sale. Anything available for sale had to be bought, since food and other goods were so hard to find. Standing in line for hours, four to five people abreast, in heat, rain, or cold, was a good way to understand the feelings of the people. They bitched at no one in particular. They had to keep it vague; being specific about the reason we endured this situation was to blame our "illustrious communists," and that was perilous. Occasionally I would hear some good jokes about our communist government:

The Prime Minister asks Ceausescu (our Stalinist leader) to open up the borders and let people explore the West. Ceausescu replies, "Are you crazy? Then there would be only the two of us left in Romania." The Prime Minister responds, "Perhaps only you."

If you inquired of your friend how he was doing, the answer would be, "Worse than yesterday, but better than tomorrow."

They (the government) pretend to pay us, and we pretend to work.

This last joke explained why there were all those shortages. Since everyone worked for the government and the government provided for everyone, there was no correlation in people's minds between hard work and the availability of goods. And without a proper incentive to work, why work at all?

My parents, like the rest of the population, hoarded food and other hard-to-find staples. You never knew when the stuff would be available again. It was common not to see meat for one or two weeks at a time, sometimes even for a month or longer. Besides relying on the food available in the stores, my parents grew their own vegetables and raised hens and a couple of pigs that were butchered before Christmas to provide meat and sausages over the winter. We were lucky in that respect, because we lived in a house with a backyard where we could grow additional food.

Alcohol, on the other hand, was plentiful. I don't remember ever seeing people wait in line for it. Most of the time, there was just one kind of booze available: plum brandy. Romania had plenty of plum orchards, and the government made sure that the mind-numbing, bad-smelling, just-one-step-away-from-blindness booze was plentiful so that people could drink and forget their miserable lives.

Not only was food in short supply, but so was just about everything else, like clothes, shoes, materials, you name it. When it came to clothes and shoes, they came in many styles – sometimes as many as one. It seems all communist countries complied with a strict code of fashion designed in China, like Mao's uniform.

The fashion rage during that time was blue jeans, but they weren't available in our stores. Any kid wearing blue jeans was admired and envied. Jeans were a symbol of the West. Some kids had parents who were able to spend a month's salary to buy a pair on the black market. Mine couldn't.

Romania has a temperate climate with four seasons: for two months it's wet and cold, for five months of the year it's freezing, for two months it's wet but getting warmer, and for the rest it's warm. I always felt cold when I was outdoors during the icy weather, mostly because the poor quality of my winter shoes let my feet get cold and wet.

My city of Timisoara had a large population of Swabian Germans who had been settled in that part of Romania for centuries. Many legally immigrated, for a fee, to West Germany, which paid the fee. We considered them the lucky ones. Kids of families who had relatives in the West received parcels with blue jeans and other Western paraphernalia. Every item they received seemed as if it were from another world – heck, from another planet.

My father brought home a few knickknacks such as Gillette shaving blades, chewing gum, and a pencil sharpener he received from a friend in the US. Never in my life had I seen such things. The Gillette shaving blades (the old style) were encased in a metal container for safety. That container resembled, to my eyes, a space-age object.

The pencil sharpener, in the shape of a rabbit, was not that much different than what was available in Romania, but its packaging was incredible. The small rabbit was encased in a clear clamshell package. I opened it very carefully and kept the package intact for some time. It looked like a work of art.

The chewing gum was heavenly: the smell, the spearmint taste, and the wrapper. I kept each foil wrapper in my shirt pocket, spreading the aroma around. I was important – I had a pack of chewing gum, and I chewed each stick of gum until it turned to rubber.

These were ordinary objects in the US or in any Western country, but they were unavailable in communist Romania. And it was not only the rarity of these objects, but the eye appeal and the quality that made them so special. The Romanian-made products' eye appeal was irrelevant; consumer products were scarce, and there was no competition among similar items, if they were available in more than one style. When the state-owned retailers distributed one product unit for every two consumers, people were not choosy as long as they were able to buy them.

Consumers were certainly not particular about the produce they bought. They had no other alternative. Potatoes were covered with chunks of dirt, apples were dented, bell peppers were cracked, and so on. Meat, when available, never came prepackaged. Sides of meat arrived at the butcher, who then cut and sold one kilogram (a little more than two pounds) per person. If the butcher knew you, or you bribed him, he might let you have the cut of meat of your choice. If not, you got what you got. Meat was rarely used for grilling because it was so hard to get and expensive. Instead, we used it in stews and soups. When meat was delivered at the butcher, everything was sold, including the bones: not for the dogs, but to be used in soups for human consumption.

The quality of consumer products was abysmal. It was not apparent what shoddy work was produced in Romania or its communist sister countries until you saw products from the West. On some occasions, products made in Romania that were slated for export but not sold abroad were returned to Romania and available to us on the retail market. They were definitely better made; otherwise no consumer in the West would have bought the junk.

For example: A meat grinder was an essential tool when you raised your own pigs and butchered them for food. My parents owned a cast iron meat grinder made before the war, but it was worn out, so my father had to buy a new one. The meat grinders made during communism couldn't grind water without breaking down. My father was happy to buy a "for export" meat grinder, made in Romania from cast aluminum. It was sleek, it was modern, and it ground meat well enough when you turned the handle, of course. But even this "for export" grinder was deficient, not because of its manufacturing quality, but because of its design. My father ended up making a few brass washers for it to make it last longer.

The problem with product quality had to do with the lack of competition among manufacturers and producers. All industry, agriculture, distribution, and retailing were owned by the state. There were no private shops. Certainly, one-man enterprises existed, but they barely survived the taxes imposed on them.

The lack of competition was a byproduct of central planning by the communist government. For example, if there were five meat grinder factories in Romania, they were all under the same ministerial umbrella and did not compete with each other. They did not have to. The government told them how many meat grinders to produce per year, and, if they met their quotas, they were heroes of the communist cause and received a pat on the back for their efforts.

How does a communist factory meet its quota? By cutting every corner and producing poor quality products so it can manufacture the number of units ordered. Domestic consumers had no choice but to accept what was given to them, whenever it was given to them.

The scarcity of products was another result of the communist command-and-control economy. The ministerial committees that decided what and how much to produce every year made arbitrary decisions based on little knowledge of supply and demand. If Ceausescu decided to show the world, or at least the communist world, that Romania was the biggest producer of cardboard shoes, come hell or high water, Romanian factories would produce an abundant number of cardboard shoes that nobody wanted or needed.

Because of shortages, stealing increased – not stealing from the public, but stealing from government institutions, and it was the employees who did the pilfering. The population did not regard their place of employment as belonging to them, to the people. The government owned everything, and they were the great exploiters now. Stealing from one's job was a kind of distorted payback. Stealing mostly took place from the food processing factories, especially the abattoirs. Meat was scarce, so the employees, through creative accounting, stole as much as they could. The stolen meat was exchanged for other hard-to-get goods or sold for premium prices.

A truck driver who did not take a trip that was on his manifest would sell the unused gasoline to automobile drivers. Flour, sugar, cooking oil, and yeast were stolen from bakeries, and the missing supplies were declared spoiled and unfit for human consumption. Canned goods or feed corn or anything edible found their way into the willing hands of buyers on the black market. Buyers were from all walks of life, including low-ranking party members. They, too, lived a life of scarcity.

You could find just about everything on the black market, for higher prices, of course. Knowing who was trafficking in the black market was valuable information. You would have to inquire among friends about such marketeers. Having connections and knowing whom to contact meant eating well that night, but with a lighter wallet. The secret police were on the lookout for the marketeers, too, considering that most goods were stolen. It was a cat and mouse game.

A funny story illustrates how cunning people were at pilfering: As it was its policy, a light-industrial manufacturer of metal and wood products insisted that, at quitting time, every employee had to exit through the guarded gates and be searched to discourage theft. One worker obtained permission from the factory director to take home wood chips left over from the wood processing. Every day at quitting time, he passed through the gates with a wheelbarrow full of wood chips. And every day, without fail, the guard inspected the load to make sure this employee wasn't hiding a stolen object in the pile, but the guard never found anything but wood chips. Eventually, both the employee and the guard retired at the same time and, on their way home on their last day of work, they decided to celebrate over a drink at a nearby tavern. After a drink or two, the guard shared that he had a feeling that the employee was stealing something, but he could never catch him red-handed. The employee, being in a cheery mood – and retired – confessed: He was stealing wheelbarrows.

The "for export" cachet was ingrained in people's minds to make them proud of making products for export. Romania, just like all the other communist countries, was in dire need of hard currency like the mighty dollar. It's interesting that "Imperialist America" had currency that even communist countries needed! It was another puzzle for me: Why did the best government system in the world (communism) need American dollars? At that time I didn't know that a currency is as good as the country that vouches for it.

My dad heard a story from a friend about a big fiasco associated with "for export." The government was in the process of building a large refrigerated storage plant for exporting pork. This plant required specialty tubing for refrigeration, which was not available in Romania or the communist bloc. The tubing was available from West Germany, and so they had to purchase it

28

from the *evil capitalist* country. After the plant was completed and they started the refrigeration system, the tubing burst.

The indignant Romanian plant director called on the German tubing manufacturer's representative. The director berated the German about selling such poor quality tubing, and, to make his point, the director said, "In Romania, when we build something for export, it is of the highest quality."

Calmly the German replied, "First, I sold you what your engineers requested. They did not ask me what the optimum tubing was for refrigeration. If they would have, I would have recommended a different type, which was not that much more expensive."

"But . . . but . . . but this tubing was for export," sputtered the director, trying to make his case.

"In Germany, we do not differentiate between products for export and products for domestic use. Every tube is made to the highest quality to comply with the standard governing that particular product. And frankly, if we would have a better quality for export, we would not export the best stuff out of Germany. We would keep it for ourselves."

I don't know if that was an "aha" moment for the director, and it did not matter. But it was an "aha" moment for my dad, and that's why he told me the story. Imagine a country that keeps the best stuff for itself! Not in communist Romania, that's for sure. The refrigeration plant was being built to freeze pork that was to be exported to countries like West Germany. Would the pork ever be available for Romanians? Only if the Germans did not want it.

Our communist government was eager to industrialize the country, a commendable action on its part. That's why Romania

29

was selling everything it could on the foreign market to earn hard currency. With that currency, government officials were able to buy the industrial components they so wanted. Unfortunately, good modern industry was expensive, but for pennies on the dollar there was much that was obsolete that capitalists were replacing and were glad to sell to communist countries for a better price than scrap metal. Romania industrialized, but with yesterday's technology, because the bureaucrats in charge of buying had no knowledge of a market economy nor the expertise to distinguish a good business deal from a bad one.

Another endemic problem with the communist government was its paranoia about espionage. We were told that Western spies were constantly infiltrating our country to obtain our industrial secrets. We were continually reminded, "Be vigilant, very vigilant." We were paranoid about spies – capitalist spies, of course. In retrospect, Romania didn't have many trade secrets to steal, and a lot of its industrial equipment was procured from the West anyway.

Paranoia kept the engineers designing the refrigeration plant from telling the German salesman what the tubing was needed for. They could have bought the right tubing the first time. Instead, the German company sold the Romanians another batch of tubing, this time for more money, and the engineers ended up in jail. Others who made bigger mistakes ended up in front of the firing squad. Retribution is harsh when you fail in communism.

4. MIND CONTROL AND THE POLICE STATE

But life went on. At school, we continued our daily classes in Marxism-Leninism and political correctness, with lessons to make us the ideal communists who would die with guns in our hands on the barricades, defending communism or conquering and transforming the world into a communist heaven. Their intent was to change us into robots that were told what to do, executing orders without complaints or thinking.

The Romanian media, completely under communist rule, did their best to brainwash us through the radio, TV, and the press. The party controlled the newspapers, and only what the communists wanted us to know was written in those newspapers. If a person published an illegal underground newspaper, that person was as good as dead. No opinion but the party line opinion was allowed.

In the early 1960s, they had an easier time showing us how glorious and advanced communism was, after the Soviet Union's success in space. The United States was that evil empire out there, inept and incompetent, intent on destroying humanity. But our closely held opinions changed for good after the US landed first two astronauts on the moon. Unbelievable! Neil Armstrong's first steps on the moon were televised live in Romania. I remember watching it in the wee hours of the morning. Was that for real? It was. The Americans did it. America had to be the superior country.

The Soviet Union and its lackluster space program became the butt of jokes after the Americans took the lead in space. What impressed us most was the openness with which the Americans showed their space program, its successes and failures, unlike the Soviet Union, which broadcast its successes after the fact and kept its failures a secret, in the true communist spirit.

The communists used the Vietnam War as negative propaganda against the United States. They had plenty of material, all from the US, to show us the war atrocities in Vietnam. But that had the opposite effect on us: The impressive technology used by the American military was awesome, although we saw the human suffering of those caught in the middle. And the US was fighting the communist North Vietnam, another hellhole like Romania. Unlike the rest of Western opinion, which was anti-American because of the war, we either didn't care or quietly sympathized with the US in their effort to stave off communism. Every time communism took a beating we cheered, hoping that one day our nightmare would end.

Romanian TV was more than happy to show Jane Fonda and her visit to North Vietnam, protesting against the evil war unleashed by her country. We took Jane Fonda and her propaganda for what it was: bullshit. My father had even stronger words for her actions. Of course, at that time, I didn't know about Hollywood's affinity for communism. What do you expect from feeble minds living in a make-believe world and thinking that communism is the world's savior? I wished they could spend a day in our shoes.

We did not love war nor want to see people die, but we sure wanted to see communism destroyed. In spite of the communist propaganda during those times, most of us did not hate the United States, but looked to it as a sign of hope for freedom in the world, even if it meant war.

Communist Romania was such a bleak place to live that most families had only one child. With a low birth rate and low life expectancy, the Romanian population decreased under communism. I was the only child in my family until my sister was born in 1968, when I was fifteen. She was one of "Ceausescu's children." In communist Romania there was no birth control of any kind, except for abortions. Women relied on abortions to stop having children, and it was not uncommon for a woman to have twenty or more abortions in her lifetime. In many cases, women put their health at risk to stop bringing children into a miserable life under communism.

Because Romania's population was decreasing, Ceausescu banned all abortions in the late 1960s. Without this birth control of last resort, women started having children, and my parents, too, had my sister. At first, the population increased, but soon people learned other methods of preventing pregnancies, and illegal abortions increased in number as well. Doctors who performed abortions were jailed. Women learned how to perform abortions on their own, and many died because of infections. Families that couldn't abort their fetuses gave birth to their children and then put them in orphanages. The Romanian population of unwanted children exploded, but communist Romania needed people, regardless of the cost to its existing population.

The police were to be avoided as much as possible. A cop could stop anyone for any reason and ask any questions, including demanding your ID and what business you were conducting at that moment. It was not uncommon for a cop to search the trunks of motorists that he stopped. No one was safe from the police.

One time my grandmother became ill, and my mother had to travel to her hometown to check on her mother. My dad and I took her to the train station for the late-night express train. On our way back from the station, not too far from our street, the police stopped us. An officer in front of us shined his flashlight in our eyes and demanded to see our IDs. I was too young to have an ID, but my father produced his. Behind us were two additional policemen, standing there to prevent us from running away. A man and a kid out late at night arose suspicion. My dad was questioned about what we were doing at that late hour, and my dad had to tell him where we had gone and that we were returning home. Since we were in our neighborhood they were satisfied that my dad was telling the truth, and they let us go.

Private-line telephones were rare at one time. My dad was able to have one installed because of his job. Later on, phones became more common, bringing the convenience of modern communication to most people. What we suspected was that the secret police could eavesdrop on a conversation, but what we didn't know was that the microphones in the mouthpieces of all telephones were rigged so that the secret police could listen in on all conversations taking place in that room. Any household with a telephone was being bugged, 24/7. That's a police state for you.

The indoctrination to behave, speak, and think like a communist happened in all aspects of daily life: from the media – praising Nicolae Ceausescu as if he were the second coming – to mandatory meetings during work or school and the specific Marxist-Leninist classes we had to attend. It seemed as though communism was all around us like a wet blanket. You could not even fart without someone taking notice of it and approving or disapproving the act of flatulence.

School was the perfect place to mold and brainwash us into becoming ideal communists. Even the way we dressed could raise the ire of some teachers. One time, a student wore an overcoat with unusual buttons: They weren't round but elongated, in the shape of a football, and made of leather. The young boy was very proud of his overcoat, but a teacher of political and constitutional sciences took offense at the coat. The man stopped him in the corridor and berated him for wearing such an outlandish garment. It was the buttons that really upset him, and he proceeded to unbutton the kid's coat, take it off him, and throw it on the floor. He sent the boy home, demanding he return only when his coat had the right, round buttons. I saw the kid a few days later, wearing the same coat with round buttons.

This kid's parents had gotten him a stylish, modern overcoat, and they probably were very proud of his attire. The political teacher's sensibility was offended by such a display of overcoat abnormality and Western influence. The communist-indoctrinated teachers picked on the smallest things that were out of the norm to make sure that we followed the communist rules, even when it came to buttons.

5. IT WAS THE MUSIC

One thing the communists couldn't stomach was rock 'n' roll. It was the ultimate decadent Western music, invented to corrupt young minds, especially the minds of young communists. Try as they might, though, the music was too good to be banned from our ears. As I later learned, rock 'n' roll was an issue with the establishment even in the West. But behind the Iron Curtain, it was considered a downright foreign, capitalist invasion.

I can see how some lyrics, with their rebellious undertone, would upset the establishment and embolden English-speaking youth to become radicalized, but for us, the lyrics were meaningless. We did not understand English. We just liked the music, the beat, and the fact that it came from the West and the communists prohibited it. What do kids do when something is forbidden? They do it.

The thing about Western music at that time was that it was much more melodic and rhythmic than other types of music we knew. The generic music available in Romania was no match for Western music. Young people fell in love with rock 'n' roll, so rock 'n' roll conquered the world. I daresay that music became one of the most important catalysts of anti-communist feelings among the youth.

Western rock 'n' roll records were not available for sale in stores, nor were they played on Romanian TV or radio stations.

The youth had no other alternative but to tune into foreign radio stations to hear the music. Two of the most popular were the Western European stations Radio Luxembourg and Radio Free Europe. We all wanted to be rebels, so we listened to those stations.

Radio Free Europe, broadcasting in Romanian, was a Western propaganda station. Music was only part of its program; the rest was political. The youth, drawn in by the music, started listening to the political programs as well. It was illegal to listen to Radio Free Europe, but just about everyone did anyway. Any customer buying a radio in a store tuned into Radio Free Europe before buying the radio to ensure that it got good reception of that particular station.

My dad listened to Radio Free Europe, and I listened along with him. Did it influence me? Of course. It was also a source of fresh information about Romania and the world, without communist censorship or ideological spin. It made us more and more aware of what a cesspool we lived in. And I paid attention to the political conversations my dad and his friends had. If a communist informant had heard them, they would have ended up in prison.

In spite of my feelings toward the communist state, I kept my mouth shut and did not show any signs that I was of another mind, except among my friends who shared the same sentiments. And since I had no chance of any other life, I had to make the best I could of it in Romania, thinking one thing and saying another.

6. HOW TO INTIMIDATE THE POPULATION

Once, a student in my school "stepped out of line" and got caught. When you're a teen and experience public humiliation such as this student did before being taken to a re-education camp, you either harden your hatred toward the establishment or cower in fear.

Romania, like all the other Central European communist countries, received plenty of Western propaganda via radio. The three notable propaganda broadcasts were from Radio Free Europe (the most popular), Voice of America, and the BBC, each transmitting its programs in a country's language. The Soviet Union had a similar propaganda station, but nobody listened to its crap. The political, news, and music programs aired by the Western stations were like a cool breeze to those stranded in hell.

Unlike North Korea, where radios can receive only stations broadcast by the state, in Romania the radios had all the AM wavelengths available in the West. We were able to listen to stations from outside Romania. I would say that nine out of ten youngsters, like myself, listened to the news and political editorials besides listening to the rock 'n' roll music. We liked what we heard, it rang true, and our political views were reshaped by these broadcasts.

Anti-communist letters smuggled out of Romania, or occasionally letters escaping the post office police censorship, were sent to Radio Free Europe. The commentators at the radio station were more than happy to read these letters on air. Of course, the commentators were careful not to mention any incriminating evidence of the sender's identity. It was good to hear the thoughts and sentiments of other dissidents like myself.

This particular student from my high school had sent such a letter, which was unflattering toward the dictator Nicolae Ceausescu. The secret police (called the *securitatea*) somehow managed to trace down the student's identity. He was to become an example in our school of what not to do. Ever.

One day the entire high school was summoned to the auditorium. We didn't know what it was about, but rumors had it that so-and-so had done something "bad." Five hundred students were crammed into the auditorium, and it was standing room only. The stage had a table draped in red (the communists' color), chairs, and the obligatory water carafes and glasses. Soon after, the principal, the assistant principal, and a thug sat down at the table. The thug glared hatefully at us and poured water in his glass. That meant he was going to give us a long sermon, a ration of communist manure. We knew the drill. It happened frequently, whether we had misbehaved or not, and we were overdue for a class in "political correctness." Yes, the communists invented political correctness so that you could express yourself only in the approved manner.

In Romania, all professionals occupying positions of importance, such as the intelligentsia, military and police officers, managers, and even teachers, were automatically enrolled in the communist party, which employed thousands of professional party members as well. These people were the politicians, administrators, bureaucrats, and activists. The activists were the equivalent of the "priests" of the communist

Inquisition. The activists were responsible for brainwashing, educating, and enforcing the communist doctrine. The thug at our school was one of them.

He signaled to someone with a nod, and they brought onto the stage the student who had done the "bad" thing. I recognized him; he was a senior. He looked down at his shoes, red-faced and ashamed. There was a dead silence in the auditorium. We were about to experience a public humiliation, a verbal and psychological flogging.

The principal addressed the audience: "Comrades, you were brought here to witness the confession of a subversive student, who until yesterday was enrolled in our school. This ex-student wrote a letter to a Western radio station, Radio Free Europe, insulting our precious leader, Comrade Ceausescu." She then read a transcript of the letter, which was honest and not too insulting, in my opinion but not theirs. However, if you did not use the most adulatory words when referring to Ceausescu, you were being disrespectful toward our supreme leader. "Comrades, let this be a lesson to all of you not to commit a crime like he did." (Yes, under communism, free speech was a crime.) "We have with us a comrade from the regional party headquarters. He will take the proceedings from here." The principal extended her hand, introducing the thug.

This menacing brute was a high-ranking activist. He was probably the equivalent of a political commissar, responsible for enforcing communist doctrine. He was here to act as a political prosecutor. He spoke like a low life from the hood. Many of us looked at each other and realized that we had more education at our young ages than this ruffian, who was about to preach to us. We were supposed to listen to this goon, who probably began his career by breaking the bones of dissidents during police interrogations.

He did not disappoint us – he began berating the student in the crudest language. The poor fellow was sobbing with shame, and it looked as if he were melting through the stage's floorboards. The language and the accusations the thug threw at our former classmate stunned the whole audience. Many students, especially the girls, were blushing with embarrassment. The thug went on for at least a half hour. I, along with many others, tuned out his verbal lashing, which in reality was addressed to all of us. The letter-writing student was just an excellent opportunity to intimidate us into acting the way the party decreed.

Finally the thug stopped, his shouting still resonating in the auditorium. He drank a full glass of water, and then refilled his glass. Was there more berating to come? After a minute, as if on cue, the assistant principal asked the student, "Comrade, what do you have to say to us about your treacherous act?"

The student mumbled some apologies and then he began crying, his whole body convulsing. This poor youngster was damaged psychologically for life, and many of us along with him. And for what? For expressing his feelings about the regime and the creep in charge, our leader, Comrade Ceausescu.

This, however, was only the first act. There was more to come. After the student quieted down, the second act began. Teachers were stationed among us in the audience, and they called the names of other students, boys and girls, and demanded that each one of them speak up and condemn the accused student. We had become co-prosecutors in this charade.

The teachers knew who harbored true sentiments toward the party and who were the troublemakers capable of writing similar letters. By selecting a few of the zealots, who glorified the party and berated their colleague, it gave the impression that the whole school was in agreement with the thug. If you believed in the communist cause, it was easy to condemn this fellow student, but if you did not, you had to lie convincingly. For the many students who had to speak up but did not agree with the regime, it was hard to go against their beliefs, but they had to say the politically correct words if they were to walk out of the auditorium on their own.

I remember my blood boiling with indignation about what was going on, about how the students were made to speak out against something they did not believe in. Luckily for me, I was just a freshman and not asked to speak up.

After the proceedings ended, we went back to our classrooms. The student was taken to a re-education institution for juvenile delinquents. He was probably released after a year or two, but his future was sealed. In a country where the government owned everything, once you've been blackballed, you can't get an education, and only the most menial of jobs will be waiting for you.

7. THINKING ABOUT GOING WEST

Life was grim in communist Romania. From time to time, I would hear about people migrating to the West, mostly ethnic Germans going to West Germany or Jews immigrating to Israel. The news coming back after they emigrated was not the doom and gloom portrayed by the communist propaganda. As a matter of fact, life on the other side of the Iron Curtain was good. Even better, most were able to buy a car. Owning a car during those times was the ultimate luxury for us.

I was sixteen and dreaming about going to the West, but my parents had no relatives there and no chance of emigrating. My father's maternal grandfather had traveled to the US in the 1920s for work. Unfortunately, my great-grandfather died from an illness in Detroit and so never returned home.

From time to time, my father daydreamed aloud about living in America and driving one of those big American cars, like a Buick. But beyond daydreaming, he never did anything about leaving Romania. Later, my father told me that the thought of emigrating never crossed his mind. But it crossed his son's mind, and very soon.

I had a dream one night, and it was a good dream: I was in Paris, near the Eiffel Tower, and I was free. I felt an indescribable sensation of well-being; I was free from all communist worries. And it felt so good, even after I woke up. Freedom was only possible in our dreams.

It was a fleeting moment of liberty, which soon succumbed to the reality of my life. Like it or not, I lived where I lived and life went on, which meant getting into trouble from time to time.

45

One day, I found some old documents with an interesting emblem on them: a double-headed eagle. It looked pretty and it fascinated me. Being artistic, I copied the design and showed it to my friends at school. A teacher caught me. He looked at the drawing with cold eyes and said, "Comrade Sandru, are you disseminating fascist paraphernalia?"

Oops. That sounded serious. Fascism was more hated than capitalism in Romania. Fascist paraphernalia? What was he talking about? Maybe because he knew my dad, the teacher just confiscated my drawings and warned my father about my transgression. Dad told me that the eagle with two heads was the emblem of the Austro-Hungarian Empire. Oops again. That was a no-no. I had no idea what that emblem meant before that incident. All symbols of the past were erased from our educational material. The exception was the swastika, the evil symbol of the Nazi, and we knew it from movies, especially the ones where the heroic Soviet soldier killed ninety-nine Germans single-handedly before himself dying like a hero, but not before killing the one-hundredth German. That was typical: Soviet movies depicted the Russians as the heroes who had defeated Nazism all by themselves. They never showed how they marched their soldiers into battle when they were all but assured of being killed. The life of a communist soldier is cheap and expendable.

Another time, I drew two triangles, one inverted and imposed over the other. It was a pretty symbol, and I wondered why I had never encountered it before. My dad told me that I had drawn the Star of David. So, what was that? The Jewish symbol. But draw too many of those, and I could be accused of Western Zionism, whatever that was. Communists could not tolerate any other insignias or symbols except their beloved hammer and sickle.

With another artistic friend of mine, I created a new alphabet making use of geometric symbols. It was fun to write to each other in runes that no one but us could understand. The math teacher, a communist zealot, caught me with a paper containing the symbols. I was in trouble. Again. Underground dissidents and spies to communicate with each other used secret codes. Was I part of such an illegal organization? I did my best to explain what it was, just a game using geometric symbols, and he let me off easy, with just a warning.

Being of the artsy-fartsy persuasion, I, along with others like me, was asked to paint at least one piece of art exulting the communist regime. Besides red flags, happy factory workers, smiling peasants, smoke stacks, and communist-era apartment buildings, what else was there for a good and fast subject? It occurred to me that the most common programs we saw on TV were political rallies held by our not-so-illustrious (in my opinion) leader, Nicolae Ceausescu. I painted a political rally, as seen from the podium. The crowd was a bunch of pink dots in a plaza, waving red communist and tri-color Romanian national flags, surrounded by communist-era apartment buildings and propaganda banners. It was two hours' worth of work, which brought me much acclaim. I wanted to puke over my own artwork.

I am a fantasist, so I tried my hand at writing a crime story that would be printed in the school gazette. I wrote it, patted myself on the back about the masterpiece I had just created, and submitted it for review and publishing. Good news, I was told; my story would be published soon. The time came, and my story appeared in print. Except it wasn't my original writing. That was my first taste of censorship. I must have been influenced by too many Western movies; my opus needed to be politically correct. Ergo, it was rewritten without my knowledge.

My story was a detective story. Its villain, a man, killed a woman, but she managed to leave incriminating evidence on him, and he was caught. The rewritten story changed the villain into a Western-influenced traitor and spy, whose crime was discovered by a communist-loving woman. He decided to silence her by killing her and then try to run for the border. Unfortunately for him, the courageous and heroic secret police comrades (the same guys who broke the bones of the accused in the jails) were quick to discover the culprit and arrested him at the train station near the border. He also had untold amounts of information on Romanian industrial secrets, which he planned to give to Western governments. The villain was apprehended, saving the state and the communist party from another evil-western-imperialist collaborator and traitor. My story was converted into communist propaganda. That episode affected me so much that it took me thirty years to decide to write another story, *Arboregal, the Lorn Tree*, a young adult fantasy and science fiction novel.

By the way, I wrote that early detective story by hand, because typewriters were scarce; not because of shortages, but because typewriters were regulated and controlled. They were ranked very high on the list of prohibited items, next to owning a gun. A typewriter in the hands of a dissident could be a powerful propaganda weapon; he could write his *poisonous*, anti-communist propaganda, and no one could tell who wrote it. With a few carbon sheets he could have triplicates and disseminate his misguided information even faster. A typewriter was a potent tool that could be used against the communist government. I think there was one typewriter in my school, kept under lock and key.

During summer vacations I worked menial jobs to earn pocket money. I found out that I did not enjoy manual labor; I preferred using my head. Besides, the best-paying jobs in Romania were reserved for the educated, so it was time to think about my future. In communist Romania, schools were free, if you were able to enroll. There were no private schools, only state schools. Everyone went to school for eight years at the primary and secondary levels. After that, there was high school. However, while primary and secondary schools were open for everyone, high school places were limited. Central planning at work!

Unlike in the US, where kids are encouraged to finish high school or get a higher education, in communist Romania the first cut was before high school. Why? Romania needed laborers. It needed educated workers as well, but, since the government employed everyone, it regulated how many type of jobs were available and what level of education was needed. Consequently they planned accordingly. There was no need for an abundant population of high-school-educated people with no working skills.

To enter high school, one had to pass rigorous written and oral exams in Romanian language, mathematics and history. Kids who could not pass the exams would go to work at age fifteen or enroll in trade schools. Realistically, not everyone needs to study to be a rocket scientist or philosopher, and trade schools, which lasted two years, were good alternatives. In communist Romania, however, going to trade school and becoming a skilled worker was not held in high esteem; it was seen as just one step above being an unskilled laborer. And this was the government of the proletariat!

For my parents and me, a higher education was the only way to go. One year before the high school entrance examinations, my parents hired tutors for me in Romanian language and mathematics, and I studied to the best of my ability to get into high school. The high school I applied to had one place for every six applicants. Unlike in the first eight years of schooling when a student went to the school in their neighborhood, a student could apply to a high school anywhere. If you think one in six is a high ratio, think again; there were more prestigious schools that had ten or more applicants for every seat. Luckily, the high school of my choice was in my neighborhood; as a matter of fact, it was the same school I had attended the previous four years.

I was serious about my education because I wanted an easier and better life in the future. I received the fourth highest score on that exam, so I secured my place in high school. What happened to the other five out of six applicants? Work, trade school, or waiting another year at home and applying for high school again. My best friend, Pal, was able to get in another high school the second time he applied. And my girlfriend at that time did not succeed the first time, either. The second time, she applied to a high school in a nearby town where the competition was less intense. After she was accepted at that school, she became my ex-girlfriend. Distance, you know.

A couple of years passed; in 1970 I turned seventeen, and in two years I would finish high school and try to enter the university. In the Romania of my times, first grade started at the age of seven years old, not six like it is today. At seventeen I was about to enter my junior year in high school, or the eleventh grade. September of 1970 approached, and school would begin once again.

After two years in high school I needed to get serious about the university entrance exam. It was time to put the radical, anarchist, hate-the-communists, liberal ("conservative" was the word used for communist lovers) me on the back burner. It was time to shape up.

I was a B student. I could have done better, but did not try. However, to get into the university, I had to pass another major exam, and the competition was even more brutal, with at least ten applicants for each place. To prevent less qualified students from entering higher education, the university entrance requirements consisted of the examination grade plus grades from the last two years of high school. That wasn't too much different than it is in the US when applying to prestigious universities. No student with B grades or lower could succeed, even if they passed the exam with an A+. It was time to up my grades to B+ or better.

You may wonder, what's the big fuss about getting a higher education? Despite the fact that communism portrays itself as the proletariat paradise, unskilled workers were paid less than educated employees. And although the pay was the same whether you worked in a factory, or a field, or an office, life was more pleasant indoors. Working in an office required a high school diploma. Making "big" money was reserved for university graduates, the intelligentsia. The work they did was mostly the thinking kind of work – fluff work with no accountability or responsibility.

The government set the salaries paid to all workers. The less skills you had, the less money you made. Educated professionals, management, and communist political activists made the highest salaries. The difference between the lowest salary and the highest one, based on education, was not that great, from the lowest salary of 800 lei to 5,000 lei for directors (company presidents) or academics. However, the quality of life was immeasurably better for professionals.

Romania is cold in the winter, and rainy and muddy in the spring and autumn. Factories were not heated, outdoor work was miserable, mechanization was scarce, and power tools were rare. Manual work was hard. In short, since the state planned and dictated everything, there were very few options for what you could do in life, as you will see shortly in my story. The only way to get to relative prosperity was through higher education.

During the summer before my junior year in high school, I went to work in a produce-crates repair shop with my best friend, Pal. Both of us were juniors but in different schools, and he was one year older than I was. Pal and I hit it off really well that summer, going to work together, to the movies, and to dances to meet girls.

Pal and I played our guitars together. He had a real one, but I had to make my own since my parents would not buy me a guitar, and my summer wages were not enough to buy one. We even started writing songs. We dreamed about starting a rock 'n' roll band. Starting a band was beyond our financial capabilities; I couldn't afford even an acoustic guitar, much less an electric guitar and amplifier. But it was good to imagine having a rock 'n' roll band or starting a band in the West, like in America, where every kid played in a band and they were making millions. Futile as they were, these dreams sustained us through those times.

8. THE REVOLT

Summer was soon over, and school began in September. Part of our "patriotic duty" in high school was to perform voluntary work during the first two weeks of school. It was not voluntary, it was mandatory, but trying to get out of it was useless, unless a doctor excused you for medical reasons.

The school gathered all the boys, loaded us into open trucks, and took us out into the country. The same thing happened with the girls, but they took them elsewhere. We all accepted the concept of the "voluntary" work. It was meant to give us an idea of what manual labor was all about, especially for us city boys. It helped us to establish camaraderie among ourselves, living together as we would for two weeks, and we were helping our country, or so we were told.

A new hog ranch was being built in the countryside, "for export" of course. The foundations for the buildings needed digging, and seventeen-year-old boys with strong backs were required. Heck, they didn't pay us, but they gave us room and board, and we were too naïve to know the difference.

Unlike the year before, when we were taken to a large house with big dormitories, this time we were taken to a couple of barracks. Each barrack served as a dormitory with dozens of beds crammed inside. The first barrack had beds with blankets and all its windows intact. The second one, where I ended up, had beds with mattresses but no blankets and a few broken windows, allowing plenty of fresh country air to blow in. We expected blankets to be delivered by that evening.

We also expected warm meals, but, instead, we were given cans of some kind of greasy stew, can openers, and spoons, one can for two boys. We ate the cold meal, grumbling about the primitive and unappetizing dinner, but none of our escorts, physical education teachers at the high school, gave a damn about our bellyaching.

Evening came, and no blankets were delivered. At 9 p.m., with the power cut off, we had to go to sleep. Romania is located at the same 45-degree parallel as Canada. Nights in September are cold, and sleeping on a bare mattress was miserable. In the morning we woke up stiff, cold, and harboring unpatriotic feelings. A bun was our breakfast; fortunately, it was one bun per student.

Soon it was time to start work, digging trenches for the foundations. We were taken to a place where markers delineated our work area. A tractor pulling a trailer arrived loaded with pickaxes and shovels. My group from the blanketless, windowless barrack was in no mood for work.

"You know what?" I said to Ned, a classmate with similar anti-communist feelings. "If this is the way they're going to feed us and house us, I'm not working."

"Me neither," he replied.

"Guys," I said, addressing the rest of our group. "I think we shouldn't lift a finger until they give us better food and blankets." Many of the boys around me nodded in agreement.

"I suggest we go back to the barracks and talk to the teachers," said Ned. That sounded like a plan, so about fifty of us returned to our barracks.

Nothing spooks the communist establishment more than mass action. They used mass action to grab power, but communists don't accept revolts against themselves. We didn't realize this at the time, but we had effectively initiated a work stoppage, a strike. Strikes are illegal in communism, under the pretext that there is nothing to strike against since there are no more rich business owners; all the enterprises are owned by the people's government, which provides the best for its workers.

The teachers who escorted us there looked stunned at our boldness. "What's going on?" asked one of them.

There was a moment of silence, when we were unsure of what to say. I was the first one to speak. "Last night I went to sleep without a blanket, and I froze. For food we're given cold, canned food and a bun for breakfast. I'm going home."

"I came here to do voluntary work, and I did not expect these harsh conditions," added Ned.

"Yes, we will not work until we are given blankets and better food," said another classmate, Ted, looking around for support among the group. Many voiced their solidarity with what he said.

The lead teacher, a muscular physical educator, turned red and approached Ted. "What did you say? All of you will stop working?"

"Yes, we will stop working until our demands are satisfied," confirmed Ted.

The next thing we saw shocked us. The lead teacher slapped Ted several times. Ted's face flushed red, and tears flowed down his face. "That's right, we are not working anymore," he repeated.

That infuriated the teacher even more, so he slapped the crap out of Ted. Between slaps, the teacher said, "So you are the leader." Slap, slap! "You instigated all this." Slap, slap!

Ted cried from the pain, and his nose bled. We were stunned seeing the brutality happening before our eyes. Teachers were not supposed to beat students, or so we thought. The teacher finally stopped. Ted was crouching on the ground, with his face in his hands.

"Anyone else want to stop working?" asked the teacher. There was silence.

What we witnessed was bizarre. We were asking for better food and blankets. Instead, one of us got beaten. Call me a blockhead, but I was not going to cower. "I'm going home," I said.

"I'm going home as well," said Ned.

The teacher who delivered the beating did not make a move toward us. A cooler-headed teacher stepped in and said, "We'll ask for blankets and more food. We'll get the blankets by tonight. I suggest you return to work." The two teachers escorted Ted inside the barrack and left us alone. We stood there, unsure of what to do. They promised they would give us blankets and better food. What else was there to do but get digging?

So we went back to work and dug. At lunch, we got hot food, and again at dinner. However, no blankets arrived. The teachers gave us some blankets that they took from the students in the other barrack, who were told to sleep two to a bed under one blanket. Blankets arrived the following day, and the situation stabilized.

Ted, the poor boy who got slapped around for speaking up on behalf of the group, was sent home. No other retribution was taken against Ned and me. The P.E. teacher who slapped Ted remained friendly toward us. Of the three of us who spoke up, only Ted got beaten. I pondered why Ned and I didn't receive the same treatment, and I concluded that it was because I had spoken up on my own behalf, not the group's, and Ned had done the same thing. Ted spoke for the group. He must have been the ringleader.

Communists are terrified of rebellion against their system. To squelch such uprisings, they are constantly on the lookout for troublemakers who might incite group rebellions. Ted was mistaken for the leader of the group and consequently was punished for it, but Ned and I started the revolt. We suffered no other reprisals during the remainder of our voluntary work.

9. BACK TO SCHOOL

We returned to classes after two weeks of voluntary work in the name of patriotism. No more goofing around for me – it was time to get serious about my studies and bring home As. And indeed I undertook my studies in earnest.

A few days after we were back in school, I was escorted to the principal's office. Being taken to the principal's office was usually for a major reason, but I was unaware of any delinquencies I had committed. In the office I found the principal, the assistant principal, and another man whom I did not know. They never bothered to tell me who he was.

The principal informed me that I was brought to her office because of my behavior during the work camp. They had conducted a quiet investigation and found out that Ned and I were the troublemakers who had incited the small, short strike. That was unacceptable behavior, and this was to be the first and last warning I would get.

I was dismayed. Asking for better food and a blanket was irrelevant to them. The fact that Ned and I were able to stir the group into action was the crime. If such behavior went unpunished, in the future I might be able to organize bigger revolts. It's better to nip the misbehavior in the bud, rather than let it flourish to its full potential. Therefore I was warned not to do that again.

The unknown man was probably from the secret police in charge of investigating any problems against the communist system. He most likely opened a dossier on me, if one hadn't been open by then. He never smiled, and he never spoke a word. He just watched.

The assistant principal then concluded that if I ever did anything like that again, besides any criminal charges (disobedience in communism is a crime), I would be blackballed and not be allowed to apply for university entrance. No university education would mean a lower standard of living for me.

I was dismissed, and I returned to classes. I talked later with Ned; he had had a similar warning in the principal's office. He told me that the police was investigating Ted's parents. Ted had relatives in the West, and his behavior gave the secret police an excuse to poke their noses into anything related to Ted's family. And the teacher who slapped Ted? He was a hero for dealing so decisively and effectively with the situation.

Oh, well. I tossed this incident into the back of my mind. I was lucky, I suppose, because I only got a verbal warning, not detention or an uncomfortable interrogation by the secret police. No more stepping out of line if I knew what was good for me. And I did behave. For a while.

I needed to improve my grades, so I studied hard, often until the wee hours of the night. My grades improved to a B+, but not much better than that. I studied even harder, but showed no improvement beyond the B+. I compared my exams with those of some classmates, including Ned, who was an A student. I saw no difference between my exams and their equivalent, better-graded exams. What was going on?

By November 1970, I realized that I was being held back. All my efforts for better grades were in vain. Was I being persecuted, quietly but very effectively, or was I imagining it? Perception is everything. I was swimming against the current. I did not like that they, the communists, were deciding my future. But there was no other alternative. Or was there?

Until the moment when I realized that I was being screwed, I looked upon defection from one's country as treason. What kind of a patriot leaves his native country for a foreign country? Only a traitor, I thought. I wanted to do my best for my country. In spite of the known fact that life was better in the West, Romania was my home. I felt that putting up with a miserable life, a lack of freedom, and all the other hardships were what a patriot was expected to endure.

I loved Romania, but communist Romania did not love me. I was a subject to be controlled, manipulated, and even sacrificed for the glory of communism. They wanted robots, not freethinking citizens. In an instant, I reversed my beliefs and decided that no country was worth giving up my freedom to take action as I deemed fit. I was not going to be cattle. Getting out of there was what I needed to do.

The question was not what to do, but how to do it. I spoke to Pal about running away to the West. He liked the idea, and soon the two of us were daydreaming of being free and famous through our music. We imagined being as famous as the Beatles and the Rolling Stones. Such hopes were frivolous and undoubtedly impossible, but it kept our spirits high while we planned our escape. The decision was made: We would seek freedom and we'd leave. Crossing the border illegally was the only way out. We could not get passports and exit visas to anywhere, especially at our age.

We needed information. How would we get to the border? What exactly was at the border? What worked, and what did not? One of the biggest problems in a communist country like Romania was freedom of movement. A citizen could not travel where he or she pleased within the country, never mind traveling abroad. And if I were to travel to another city I would have to inform the police about who I was, what my business

61

was there, and how long I'd be staying. It would be almost like traveling to a foreign country.

Going to a border town was prohibited without police permission. As a matter of fact, if I got on a train and got off in a border town, and I did not reside there or have a special permit to be there, I would be arrested. Imagine traveling from Los Angeles to Calexico, a border town with Mexico, and being arrested by police there for being a resident of L.A.!

I gathered information about border-travel restrictions from two classmates who lived in a border town and attended my high school in the city. From them I learned that border patrols watched the border from tall towers, and they patrolled the border day and night. I learned that the actual border was a strip of dirt about twenty-feet wide, finely raked for the sole purpose of seeing if anyone walked across it during the night before. That information was valuable. At least we would know when we crossed the actual border and entered Yugoslavia. The two classmates became suspicious about my inquiries, but, fortunately, they kept quiet about my interest in the border.

Crossing the land border sounded difficult and dangerous, so we considered crossing the Danube, but that route sounded even more daunting. I'd seen the Danube from the train when I had traveled to visit my grandmother in Oltenia, in southern Romania. I even swam in the river when I was a kid, and it seemed awfully wide and perilous. Another alternative was to escape along one of the rivers crossing into Yugoslavia, perhaps by swimming underwater. I was envisioning a small submersible, so we could breathe under water, and even had pipedreams about building one. Then we found out that the border-river crossings had iron gates across the rivers to prevent anyone from escaping underwater.

Neither Pal nor I warmed up to a wet crossing. The land route was our only choice. Then it was a matter of deciding where to cross. It had to be at a border town with train access. Because we were teenagers with no other means of transportation, getting there by train was imperative.

I searched for reliable maps of the border area. General maps were available, but detailed maps were not. Probably only the military or other officials had such maps, and they were beyond our reach. In the end, I managed to get into the map room at school with the help of my girlfriend Rose, and found a big enough map with enough detail to get a good understanding of the lay of the land. I meticulously traced that area of the map. That piece of paper became my only geographical reference, and from it we decided where to cross. To avoid arrest, we decided to get off the train just before the border town and then follow the railroad tracks to the border.

The remaining question was when to do it. In the winter, it was cold and snowy, and in the spring it would be too rainy and muddy. Besides, we had to wait until I turned eighteen. Pal was already eighteen, but I was not and I was afraid that if we made it across, I would be turned back from Italy or Austria for being a minor. It never crossed my mind that I might not make it that far. I would turn eighteen in May. Summer would be the only good time to escape, and July or August the best time for our adventure.

Besides our team of two, we probed the feelings of other friends to see if they would be interested in joining us. We figured the bigger the crowd, the greater the courage. So as not to raise suspicions, we approached our other friends in a hypothetical way, asking what they would think if any of us would cross the border. No one we knew well showed a desire to be jailed or shot; freedom wasn't worth the price to them. But it was to Pal and me. The only other person who knew about our plans was my girlfriend Rose.

We had high hopes of escaping and beginning a free and prosperous life in the West, until Pal came home from school one day in January and told me the horrific news. Three students from his school had attempted to cross the border on New Year's night. They figured that the border patrols were drunk and asleep, and they could more easily sneak across the border. But the patrols were wide awake. The students stepped on a trigger-wire that launched a flare, illuminating everything around them. The ground was covered with snow, and the three of them were clearly seen.

They decided to make a run for the border, which was within sight. The patrols were too far away and couldn't catch them. Instead, the guards opened fire, killing all three of them. Pal told me that the parents received their kids' clothes, riddled with bullet holes and stained with blood, but not their bodies. It chilled us. Being killed while trying to cross the border was a possibility. It was the ultimate punishment for freedom seekers. But we had thought it happened rarely. It sure dampened our resolve to escape.

I didn't know about Pal, but I reassessed my situation over the coming weeks. I had relaxed in my studies, and my grades declined. They were passable, but nowhere near where they had to be. I was convinced that I was being persecuted to prevent me from entering the university. Life was bleak, and every day it got worse and worse. I was suffocated by the unrelenting bull thrown at us every day in the media and at school about wonderful communism and the bigger-than-life Nicolae Ceausescu, our totalitarian Stalinist leader, who liked to be called "*Conducator*," the Romanian word for leader, like the German name *fuhrer*.

On the other hand, the West became more desirable day by day. Western rock 'n' roll music played a major role in bringing some relief to me and many other teenagers. Although there had been a slight relaxation of communist rule after the Prague Spring in 1968, the system clamped down on us again, with renewed attacks against the West and its evil music. One way to show our opposition to the communist regime was to attend the midnight mass at Easter. Communists are atheists, so God and religion were not part of our training. Although the communists in Romania did not outlaw the Christian Orthodox or other religions, they frowned upon the practice of any religion.

Therefore, at midnight mass on Easter, thousands of students flooded the streets and churches celebrating Christ's resurrection. Honestly, we had no idea of the importance of that religious celebration, but since the communists denied God and religion, we wanted to show how we denied communism by participating in the religious celebration. Easter was in the spring, and it was like a celebration of the free, but without any freedom.

By that spring I had made up my mind: We would cross the border and get out of this hell. The killings over the New Year did not seem as frightening anymore, and I reasoned that winter was not a good time to cross the border anyway. With snow on the ground, it was easy to be spotted, even at night. Summer was the right season, and late July was set as the date of our great escape.

But Pal got cold feet. His excuse was that he wanted to finish his studies in high school before seeking freedom. So, another year's delay was necessary. It was a bogus excuse: he was afraid. I was desperate to get out, and had burned enough bridges by now at school that I had no way of retreating. I told him that I was sorry but that I would do it alone. There was a chance that he could change his mind by summer, but my mind

65

was set. I felt that I was prepared; after all, I was the one planning and accumulating all the information necessary to cross the border. Freedom could not taste any sweeter nor be any more urgent.

10. A DIFFERENT TURN OF EVENTS

I turned eighteen in May 1971, and I became an adult. I was as determined as ever to leave, although I realized it would have been better with a friend like Pal. My grades suffered, and my parents were upset by my lack of effort to do any better. I did not care about school. I had C+ grades, good enough to pass, except for one subject, German language, which I was flunking.

I had always wanted to learn English. In Romania, children learn one foreign language starting in secondary school and a second one in high school. I was lucky that I wasn't forced to learn Russian, so I took French. In high school, I could choose between Russian or German; I took German. I was studying English on my own, and that may have contributed to my indifference toward the German language.

In late May we had finals, German language included. I hadn't studied, so the German language exam looked like Greek to me. Every student around me was diligently writing on the final exam paper. I didn't care and sat in my chair with my arms folded. The German language teacher was already not fond of me. She was an active communist agitator, lauding Ceausescu, our Fuhrer, any chance she got. I was not fond of her, either. I had managed to piss her off in the past, and she did not hide her displeasure toward me. My act of defiance, as I sat there with my arms folded, was the last straw for her.

She picked up my blank exam paper, gave me a zero grade, and told me to get out of the classroom, to the horror of the other students in the class. I took my time placing my pencil and other objects in my bag, stood up, and proceeded to the door. The teacher was patrolling the classroom, making sure that other less studious pupils did not cheat or copy from their neighbors. I was gone from her mind by the time I got up from my seat.

On my way out, I passed by her desk, and there was my blank final, with a big red zero on it. Casually, without any thought of remorse or guilt, I snatched the paper with my left hand and put it in my pocket. No one saw what I did. Now there was no exam to prove me guilty. I held back a mischievous laugh (I was a teenager after all) and got out. I had time to kill until my next class, so I just sat on a bench in the schoolyard, daydreaming about my big escape.

Ten minutes later, my classmate Ollie, who had been taking the German language final as well, came out smiling and joined me on the bench. Ollie was not a close friend, but a good classmate. He was very good friends with Ned.

"What are you smirking about?" I asked him.

"You snatched your final off her desk, didn't you?" he said.

By then I had ripped the final paper into shreds and tossed it in a trashcan. "Maybe," I smirked maliciously.

"She went ballistic when she found out what you did. If she didn't have an entire classroom taking the final, she would have come after you like a bat out of hell."

"Really?" I played innocent about eliciting such a reaction from her and changed the subject. "How come you're here?"

"She caught me copying from Ned," he said. His smile disappeared as he realized he was in deep trouble as well. "I got an F. I flunked German."

"Well, me too," I said to comfort him or to make myself feel better. "It doesn't matter. I won't be around in the fall to take the makeup exam." By that time, I thought, I would be free and away from this mess.

"No? Where are you going?" He was curious.

Well, Ollie was a friend of Ned's, and I knew that Ned shared my feelings about the communist system. I felt comfortable telling him what I was planning. "I'll be running away and crossing the border."

"When? Where?" He was very excited.

"In July or August. I'm planning to cross into Yugoslavia."

"Can I come?" Ollie asked.

I did not know what to say at first. Not many friends were willing to take the risk and come along with me. And here a classmate, but not a friend, was willing to join with someone he didn't know that well, either, to cross the communist border illegally. "Are you sure?" I asked in disbelief.

"Yes, I want to."

"You know it is dangerous," I said.

"Everything is dangerous in this country," he said, "but I'll come."

"All right." We shook hands to secure the deal. We exchanged information on how to keep in touch over the summer for our upcoming escape.

He then asked, "Once in Yugoslavia, where are you going?"

"I'm planning to go to the Italian or Austrian border and cross there. Not sure yet."

"You know, I have relatives in Yugoslavia. We could ask them to help us."

I didn't realize it then, but that was incredibly good news. Crossing the border into Yugoslavia was the most dangerous part of our escape, so most of my thoughts were concentrating on that portion of the journey. Walking across Yugoslavia was something I hadn't considered in depth. We would walk, hitchhike, or ride a train like hobos, or something. Getting help in Yugoslavia was good. "Sure, that will be helpful," I replied coolly.

11. BAD NEWS

School ended on June 15, 1971. I came home with my report card. Bad news: I had flunked German. It was the first time I had ever flunked any subject. My parents were beside themselves when they saw my report card. Never mind my other bad grades, which were passing; my final grade in German was three (out of ten points.) In the fall I would have to take a makeup exam and receive a grade of seven or better to pass, otherwise I would have to repeat the year. Seven was the equivalent of a B-.

I wasn't worried.

But my parents were. They were at the end of their rope. No more leniency toward me: no more rock 'n' roll music, bell-bottom pants, long hair (it wasn't that long), or my homemade guitar. I was going to be sent to the mountains, to some relatives in a remote village, to study and be away from all the bad influences of music, friends, and, worst yet, girls. My fate was sealed. I was going to depart that coming Saturday and stay in that village until the first week in September, before the makeup exam.

September? No way. By then the weather might be cold and rainy. My window of opportunity to cross the border in summer would be gone. I was screwed. What could I do? Only one thing: Run for the border before my parents packed me on a train to monastic living. I got in touch with Ollie and informed him that we would leave that Friday. It was the moment of truth. A definite date for our departure, and we had to take the plunge into the unknown.

I was kind of relieved when Ollie said, "OK. What do I need to do?"

"Come to the train station Friday. Get a ticket to the town of Cruceni for the 11 a.m. train. I'll meet you there." It was time to take action. Dreaming, planning, and wishing were over.

I bought a few chocolate bars and a packet of cookies for the trip. I packed them all in a Romanian hippie-style shoulder bag Rose had knitted for me. For good measure, I took a knife. I committed the map to memory before burning it for fear of getting caught with it and having it considered another strike against me. I told Rose of my departure, and she insisted on coming with me to the train station to say good-bye. I told Pal about my Friday departure and hoped that he would change his mind and come with me. He didn't. But he gave me a compass to help me out in my escape. It was nice of him.

On Friday morning, before my parents left for work, they gave me money and told me to go to the barber and get a haircut for tomorrow's departure to the mountain village. They said good-bye and left for work. I dressed, grabbed my hippie bag with my supplies in it, went to the next-door neighbors, and left the key to the house with them before leaving for the train station.

Rose was waiting for me at the station. She brought a couple of sandwiches for the trip, which I much appreciated later. I bought my ticket and went to the platform to wait for the train. We sat on a bench waiting for Ollie and the train. We kissed, and I promised her that I would return for her once I was established in the West. She promised that she would faithfully wait for me, no matter what. It was heart wrenching to see her sad face.

Ollie came onto the platform. My heart sank again. He was empty-handed. If he hadn't brought any supplies with him it was because he had changed his mind, I figured. "Are you coming?" I asked him, dreading the answer.

"Yes, I have my ticket," he said.

I felt relieved, but a bit annoyed at his lack of preparation. The annoyance quickly dissipated, however; it was better to have a partner, even an unprepared one.

The train entered the station. Ollie was smoking to calm his nerves. I was holding Rose, who started sobbing. The conductor whistled, and we boarded the train. The last thing I saw was Rose waving to me, with tears streaming down her face.

12. THE TRAIN JOURNEY

The train was moving toward our final destination. Ollie looked as pale and scared as I probably did. However, at eighteen you have hope and a bit of excitement about the adventure awaiting you. I told Ollie about the plan. We would get off at the station before the border town of Cruceni, follow the railroad tracks to the border, and cross it somewhere there.

But things don't always happen according to plan, in spite of my absolute trust in it. The border is only fifty miles from Timisoara, but the train was slow and stopped at every station, making the ride several hours long. We were approaching the third station from the border, when Ollie, who was smoking in the corridor, sounded the alert. "Cops, two of them, checking IDs."

That was big trouble. The police did not wait until passengers got off the train at the border town; instead they asked for IDs while in transit. They were advancing toward us as they were checking the passengers' IDs.

"Let's walk toward the rear," I said. We casually walked away from them. "If the train doesn't stop before they catch up with us, we'll have to jump off the train," I told Ollie. There was no other way.

But the train stopped before the police entered the last car where we had taken refuge, so we got off. This train station was just a two-room building in the middle of nowhere. There were no towns nearby, and outside there was plenty of daylight. It was too early to head for the border. We sat on a bench and ate the sandwiches Rose had given me. Thank God for her thoughtfulness. We needed the nourishment.

After an hour or so we exited the station and surveyed the countryside. Incredibly, we could make out where the border was. The watchtowers were clearly visible on the horizon. There was no need to follow any tracks; we just had to walk toward the skeletal towers. So we took a dirt road headed toward them. The only soul we met was a farm-tractor driver who was sleeping near a haystack with the tractor's engine running. Welcome to communism: His boss may have thought, by the engine's noise, that he was working; instead he was catching a nap.

It was now after eight o'clock in the evening. The road curved away from the border. It was not a good way to go; the watchtowers were our destination on the horizon. We departed from the road and entered a golden wheat field. The wheat was up to our waists, and we walked two abreast, leaving a wide trail in the field. The sun was nearing the horizon, although at that latitude darkness wouldn't come until ten o'clock at night. Ahead of us, against the low sun, we saw a man riding a horse.

"Down!" I said to Ollie. We dropped down low in the wheat.

"What's the matter?" he asked.

"Horseback patrol." I recognized the gun pointing up on his back. In the middle of the wheat field, we were like two flies in a bowl of cereal. Fortunately for us, the border guard was doing his rounds watching the fields toward the border. If we had been a half hour earlier and passed his patrol road, he would have spotted us from behind and our escape would have been over. Even now we were in danger, as the path he rode on was elevated, and, being on horseback, he had a good vantage point over the fields around him. All he had to do was look over his shoulder and see two trails in the wheat field that ended abruptly. We were easy pickings there.

But it was his job to watch the border, not the fields toward the interior of the country. As we progressed with our escape, we were learning as we went along. There was no sense in continuing as long as there was daylight. Another patrol could have come along and seen us. We lay down in the wheat field until the sun set. At dusk, when we considered it safe to get up, we started again toward the border. We crossed the road where we had seen the border patrol and, for a moment, we wondered if that was the border, the fine strip of land I had heard about. But it was just a dirt road.

We crossed it and entered into another wheat field. It was getting dark, and the towers were barely visible in the dim light. I tried to use my compass, the one Pal had given me. It had a phosphorescent needle and was visible in the dark. I had never used a compass before to orient myself, and it didn't seem to do us any good. We were walking in complete darkness, hoping that we were heading in the right direction.

During the day the weather had been fair, but as it got dark we didn't notice the heavy clouds that were rapidly covering the sky. It started raining. There we were, two city boys in the middle of a wheat field, without any rain gear or warm clothes, far away from any town. The heavens opened up. It began raining so hard that we couldn't keep our eyes open from the water drenching us. Occasional lightning illuminated the wet hell around us. The wheat surrounding us was beaten down to the ground by the rain, and we stumbled on the thick carpet of fallen wheat. The wind blew so furiously that – I think now – we might have been near a small tornado.

We were drenched, cold, and lost in an open field with no shelter in sight. Even if there had been shelter nearby we couldn't have seen it anyway. This was pathetic. We were not stopped by the border patrols, but by the weather. We stumbled along because we couldn't see three steps in front of us. At times

Ollie and I even held hands so as not to lose track of each other. It was a miserable situation.

Suddenly, the rain stopped, not a drop anymore, but the wind began in earnest. We were like two lost, wet cats. Now my compass was really useless; as I shook it, I could hear water sloshing inside it, and the phosphorescent needle was stuck. The wind blew mercilessly, chilling us to the bone. Frankly, we lost hope and were about to succumb to hypothermia. Arrest would have been a welcome outcome. We were that desperate.

I squatted down to keep warm, and nearby I spotted several humps. "Haystacks!" I yelled. Those haystacks were the most welcoming sites. "We need to bury ourselves in one of them," I told Ollie, and we ran to one.

It was wet on the outside, but we buried ourselves inside the haystack. It was the most pleasant feeling to escape the chilly wind and feel the warmth of the hay. Deep inside it was dry, and it smelled like grasses. Soon our bodies' heat and the insulating hay warmed us up. After we stopped trembling and felt good again, I shared a chocolate bar and a few cookies that were not soggy with Ollie. We didn't know where we were, but we were still in Romania; we hadn't crossed the border yet. Tiredness overtook us, and we fell asleep. Tomorrow would be another day.

Much later I found out what had happened at home with my family. My parents had no idea about the journey I had started. As far as they knew, I left home to get a haircut. They inquired with our neighbors, who said that I had left with my hippie bag around my shoulder to go to town. As it got late they began to worry, because I had never missed coming home at night in the past. They agonized all night, waiting and hoping that I would come home.

13. SECOND DAY, SATURDAY

We woke up the next day to a sunny morning. You wouldn't have known that the night before we had almost drowned standing up in the rain. The weather was nice and warm, which helped get our clothes completely dry. I emptied my wallet of mostly pictures of Rose and spread them on the grass to dry them.

The haystack where we had found shelter was near a deep ditch. It could have been for irrigation or drainage, but it was parallel to the border. We were on the bank closer to the border, so we wouldn't have to traverse it and get wet again. On the opposite bank an old peasant woman walked by. We exchanged good mornings and hoped that she would not report us to the police. We had "city boys" written all over us.

It was time to move on. The watchtowers were close by. They were easily sixty to seventy feet high, and we had no doubt that the patrols stationed at the top would be able to see us with binoculars. We walked toward the border on a dirt road flanked by wheat fields. It was obvious that on the brown road we were somewhat camouflaged, but in the wheat field we could be spotted instantly.

"Ollie, we need to find shelter," I told my friend. "They'll catch us if we continue like this."

"But where?" he asked.

The wheat field was wide, as far as the eye could see. From place to place there were clumps of thorny bushes, and one of them of a medium size was to the left of us. "We need to hide in those bushes," I indicated with a nod of my head. We crawled under its canopy, trying not to get pricked by the thorns or have them snag or rip our clothes. Near the stubby trunk we found a space large enough that we could sit or lie down in it comfortably without being seen from the outside. It was a good place to hide. We were in the shade and all we had to do was wait. At dusk we would be able to approach the border without being detected.

***

It was Saturday morning. At home my parents were really panicking, fearing that I had eloped with my girlfriend, Rose, or, worse yet, that something terrible had happened to me. Terrible things were uncommon in Romania at that time; crime was low, one of the benefits of a police state. My parents went to my friend Pal's house and inquired if he knew about me. He denied knowing my whereabouts. It was not necessarily for my sake as it was for his own not to talk. Having knowledge of my plans and not divulging them to the secret police was a crime. Everyone was required to be an informant.

Not having any news about me, my parents went to the police to report me missing. The local police referred my case to the secret police, since it was very rare that people would go missing because of criminal mishaps but more common that they had run away to the border.

When they came back, still debating about how to find my girlfriend's house in case I was with her, they found Pal and his mother waiting for them. Pal's mother had forced him to spill the beans and rat me out. He told them that I'd run for the border. Rumor has it that my mom's anguished scream was heard for several blocks. Attempting to cross the border meant jail at best, death at worst, and either way a definitely ruined future.

The secret police officer wasted no time in visiting my parents. At this point he was still gathering evidence about me, so he was gentle with my parents: First interrogate with kindness, and then, if that does not work, begin an ever-increasing coercive interrogation. My parents were innocent of any knowledge of my actions. Also, I was an adult now.

After he gathered all the information he could, the officer went to talk to Pal. He was not so gentle with him, threatening him with arrest and jail for being an accomplice to a traitor like me. The police scared him into telling everything he knew, even the little he knew about my accomplice, Ollie. They interviewed all my neighbors and all my friends in the neighborhood. These other people knew far less or nothing about what I had planned, and so the police left them alone.

Rose suffered similar rough verbal treatment from the secret police. She must have been credible in her denials, though, because there were no repercussions against her. Pal was not charged, either, maybe because Pal's dad had been a cop, though not in the secret police.

The moment the secret police found out that we headed for the border they informed the border patrol about us. However, they did not know where we were or even if we had crossed it the night before.

***

In the fields it was dusk, and the time had come to get up and attempt the crossing. We came out from under the bush cautiously and located the watchtowers. They were an excellent point of reference. We took a dirt road nearby toward them, but soon it ended at another irrigation ditch that ran parallel to the border. There was no other way but to cross the stinky, muddy, leech-infested water. We took our shoes and pants off and descended the steep banks into the water. The water was only waist-deep and about ten feet wide. Carrying our shoes and pants above our heads, we crossed it quickly, feeling the occasional leech attempting to have dinner on us. On the other side, getting up the steep bank had its challenges, but we managed.

I had been told that sometimes the border-side banks of the ditches were wired with tripflares. The bank we climbed on was clear, and we saw why. There were more agricultural fields between this ditch and the border. This time we were in a cabbage patch. They looked like heads perfectly lined up, but the rows ran slightly at a diagonal to the border. Following the rows of cabbages would not have led us to the border, but just to the left of it.

We proceeded along the rows of cabbages, hunched down and keeping as low to the ground as possible. However, every so often we moved laterally to the right to keep a true course to our destination. I even counted how many rows we skipped in case we needed to get back to our original point of reference. The cabbage patch ended, and a field of freshly cut hay opened up toward the border.

The field seemed to be about six hundred feet wide, ending in a hedge of bushes. The towers were located beyond those bushes. That field looked like a no-man's-land. If I ever felt exposed during this endeavor, it was in this field. Even in the dark we resembled two sacks of potatoes lying on the ground.

We couldn't wait. We could barely make out the watchtower ahead of us. It was our only point of reference, and without it we were lost. We lay down and began crossing the field on our bellies. That was a nasty undertaking. We were not soldiers and didn't know how to crawl properly. On top of that, the short-cut grasses were not soft, and they pricked our tender spots. We advanced slowly, and it was getting darker.

It seemed to be quiet around us, so we decided that crawling on our bellies was silly. We stood up and, bent at the waist, we advanced toward the barely visible towers while keeping our ears open for patrol noises.

Suddenly, on our left, a green flare popped up into the sky. It became as bright as daylight, and we could see our shadows and everything around us. We flattened to the ground and froze. The flare was close by, almost on top of us, it seemed. We did not dare move or breath, hoping that it was not intended for us and that we were not spotted.

We lay as flat as pancakes on our stomachs in a field with nowhere to hide. We were sitting ducks. Another green flare popped farther on our left. After the pop and while the flare was still illuminating the fields, we heard a lot of commotion from that side. People yelling, dogs barking, more people yelling and screaming. Something was happening not far from us.

And then the chilling ra-ta-ta-ta-ta burst of a Kalashnikov. Oh my God! The border patrols were shooting. Who were they shooting at? We heard more yelling, orders given, shouts and screams, dogs barking again. We heard one more single pop, maybe a flare; I couldn't say since I had my eyes closed. Then all was quiet.

After a while I saw a red flare erupt in the sky, watching it from the corner of my eye, my head buried under my arms. There was major trouble; we could hear shouts coming from farther away on our left side. We tried to lie as flat as we could. The commotion from the border patrols started again. They were no farther than two hundred yards from our location. In the open field, that distance felt like two hundred feet. I did not dare raise my head and glance in the direction of trouble, I just listened with my nose buried in the grass, arms around my head. We stayed put, praying that we would not be spotted or sniffed out by the dogs. And the gunshots – what happened? Did they shoot someone? I was beginning to feel nauseated.

I, at least, was scared shitless. Were we going to be discovered next? Should we run to get away from this hot spot? Even if I could have tried to run, my legs were so weak and trembling that I couldn't even get up. Fear kept us paralyzed. It took a while but the commotion died down. From time to time we could hear voices, laughter, and shouts. Dogs were barking again, but this time it seemed that the patrols were playing with their dogs. We hoped that they would not come our way. We stayed there for perhaps another hour, until everything was completely quiet.

I found out later the meaning of the red flare. They had captured people trying to cross the border. The red flare alerted their command about the capture, and additional patrols were sent to bring the captives in. That night, people just like us attempted to cross the border nearby. Because they were caught and the patrols were distracted, we were not spotted and we remained free.

When we felt that it was safe we began crawling on our elbows and knees toward the border. We reached higher grasses and walked low to the ground, stopping from time to time to listen for any signs of patrols. The tall grasses gave way to bushes, where we could then walk semi-erect, making our walk easier. By now we were lost again, and we had no idea where the border was. We looked around, trying to orient ourselves, but it was dark and we could not make out any points of reference. After a few more steps in no particular direction, other than in the path allowed by the bushes, we saw something nearby.

To our surprise, it was a huge iron frame jutting out of the ground. We looked up and stared dumbfounded at the crisscrossing metal work of a watchtower. By chance, we had ended up underneath one of them. Cold shivers ran down my spine. It was as if we were entering the mouth of the dragon. We turned around and checked our surroundings, expecting at any moment to be looking down the barrels of Kalashnikovs. We stood there, staring at the base of the tower and wondering, "Is this good or bad? What should we do?" This was a dangerous place, but maybe not at night, I thought.

"Ollie," I whispered. "This may be the safest place around." The watchtowers were used only during the day. Unlike concentration camp watchtowers, which had searchlights, the border towers did not. At night they were unmanned. Besides, who in their right mind would get near them, even at night? Well, we were there, and it seemed the safest place in the area, and it was.

"Should we sleep here?" Ollie wondered.

"Yes, under that bush." And so we ended up in the most unlikely place on the entire border, at the base of a watchtower, where we fell asleep.

We woke up before dawn, while it was still very dark. It was quiet around us and, for some reason, I felt the need to check the time. I asked Ollie to strike a match so I could check my wristwatch. Only two dumb kids – and we were dumb – would strike a match so close to the border to find out that it was two o'clock in the morning. Being satisfied that it was a good time to get going, we left the tower base and headed for the border, or where we thought the border must be.

From my past inquiries, I knew that the watchtowers were the last line of defense before the actual border, that strip of finely raked land beyond which freedom awaited us. I didn't know how far it was, but as long as we walked away from the tower, we would find the border shortly. The grass was as tall as we were, but we found a narrow path that made the walk much easier. We walked for a good five minutes but we didn't come across the border.

"Damn it," I said. Up ahead of us another watchtower loomed in the dim pre-dawn light. We had trooped all this time on a path established by the border patrols that ran parallel to the border and connected the towers. "This way," I told Ollie, and we walked into the wall of tall grasses on our left. I knew we had come from the right, so the border had to be in that direction.

We hadn't even gone ten feet before we got out of the tall grasses and encountered a dirt road. We walked to the edge of it and looked right. It continued into the distance straight as an arrow. We looked to the left and it continued that way as well.

"Is this the border?" whispered Ollie. Together we squatted down and touched it. It was made of smooth dirt, not finely raked dirt, and it was about twenty-feet wide.

"Screw it," I said. "Let's worry about it on the other side." I crossed it, followed closely by Ollie. The dirt was smooth and muddy from the previous night's rain. The mud caked on the bottom of our shoes, but we did not care if we left tracks. We were not even sure that this was the border.

We reached the other side and looked back. The dawn arrived, and in the pale light we could see the watchtowers on the other side of the dirt strip. Behind us there were pastures of freshly cut fields all the way to the edge of the dirt strip.

"Are we in Yugoslavia?" I wondered aloud.

"I think so," said Ollie.

"But where are the Yugoslavian watchtowers?"

"I don't think they have watchtowers, like Romania," said Ollie, sounding kind of sure about this fact.

I wasn't one-hundred-percent sure we had crossed the border into Yugoslavia. "Let's go," I said, and we walked away from the strip of dirt. The field ahead of us was peppered with haystacks, and for a moment I had the crazy idea of going to sleep in one of them. But if we had crossed the border and it was so near behind us, we had better put some distance between it and us.

14. THIRD DAY, SUNDAY

After an hour of walking through the fields, we reached a one-lane cobblestone road. I was sure that there were no such roads in Romania. Son of a gun, we were in Yugoslavia! It was easier to walk on this road, and every so often it widened to two lanes. There was no traffic at this early hour. Sometime later, we walked by a small village. The words on the street signs and the few traffic signs said loud and clear, "Yugoslavia." One of the streets was called "Timisoara" after our city. It felt good to see something familiar, even if it was just a name.

We had made it. We were out of Romania. We were free, or almost free. The worst part of our trek was over, and we were successful – not in jail, not killed. The sun rose and there was a new day, Sunday. We started walking with renewed vigor. We walked and we walked, keeping watch for police cars possibly searching for us. The Romanian patrols might have discovered our shoeprints and alerted the Yugoslavian patrols and in turn the police to look for two escapees from Romania.

From time to time we got off the road to rest. We were hungry and tired, but we dared not stop for too long. One time, as we were resting, we saw a police car pass by. They were out there, maybe looking for us. We waited for a while, and, when we felt sure it was safe, we continued on the road or as near the road as possible, in case we had to run away from the police. Orienting ourselves by the sun, we trekked southwest to reach Alibunar, Ollie's uncle's village.

By midafternoon, we were exhausted and hungry. As we turned a bend we saw a police car parked on the side of the road, looking like it was waiting for us. The cop was talking to some peasants in the field as if inquiring about two suspicious characters like us. We moved to the right of the road into the tall

89

grass and waited. The cop was in no hurry, as if he expected us to appear any minute. We abandoned the road and walked through the countryside, bypassing the police car.

Most of the agriculture in that area was fields of young corn, but eventually we came across a plum orchard. The plums were not ripe yet; on one side they were purple and on the other green. Since we had finished the chocolate and cookies by now, this was the only food available to us. The semi-ripe plums tasted sour-sweet. We didn't care, we were hungry, and we ate as many as we could. An hour later both of us had diarrhea. There was no toilet paper, but at least there were plenty of green leaves.

After an arduous walk, in the evening we stopped in a small grove for the night. Although we were young and in relatively good shape, we had never walked this much before. Our shoes were street shoes, and our feet were aching. Worse yet, I felt as if a rubber band was constricting my calves, and no matter what position I tried, the pain wouldn't go away. Hunger did not improve our situation. There were no more orchards, and even if there were, we had learned our lesson with the plums.

As night descended, the temperature cooled down. We ended up trying to sleep in a sitting position, leaning against a small tree, shoulder to shoulder. We were cold, and we shivered all night while fighting the mosquitos. We took catnaps, but the morning was slow to come.

15. FOURTH DAY, MONDAY

It was our second day in Yugoslavia, and we still didn't know how far we were from Alibunar, Ollie's uncle's village, but we thought we were heading in the right direction. Knowing that we were farther from the border, we walked on the road and tried to hitchhike. It didn't work; nobody stopped to give us a ride. It may have been because we didn't know what the correct hand signal was to request a ride, such as holding an arm out with the thumb up. We were shaking our thumbs in the direction of traffic. No one stopped, and so we walked.

We were starving, because we hadn't eaten real food in days now. When you're hungry you tend to talk about food. At one point I asked Ollie, "What would you like to eat right now?"

"Beef-and-green-bean stew in tomato sauce," he replied.

He took the words right out of my mouth. "Me, too." Despite being so tired, we laughed a good laugh. Then we swallowed hard and marched on.

***

At home, on this Monday, my dad went to my school to inquire about my classmate and his parents' names and address. As it happened, Ollie's dad was there, too. My dad and Ollie's dad were not received with much sympathy from the small staff of teachers present at the school over the vacation. One teacher said, in a seemingly knowing way, that we were captured or would soon be captured. That was not good news for our dads, but there was not much to do until official word came down.

The school would have a big problem come September when classes would start. If we were successful, we would embolden other students to follow in our footsteps. The school's only hopes were that we would be caught and serve as a good example to the other students of what not to do. Freedom was forbidden.

Outside the school, Ollie's dad and my dad talked, trying to find out from each other what had happened. My dad was completely shocked by my leaving home and going to the West. Ollie's dad was dismayed about Ollie joining me to cross the border. He didn't know about Ollie's plans or about me. Unlike my family, Ollie's family was all in favor of leaving Romania. They wished they could get out legally. However, if their son could make it across the border and immigrate to the West safely, that would be great. Then, perhaps, Ollie would be able to bring them over. My dad had never thought of that possibility until then. That was also when my dad found out that Ollie's family had relatives in Yugoslavia, and that if we crossed the border we would most likely go to them, asking for assistance. At least there was a ray of hope.

***

In Yugoslavia, whenever we stopped to get water we'd asked the folks, "Alibunar?" and they would indicate which way to go. We came to a fork in the road, and we had no idea which direction to take. Stumped, we talked to a man and tried to converse with him in French. Being high school students with seven years of French language study under our belts, we felt we could handle a conversation as simple as asking in French, "Where is Alibunar?"

For us, speaking French was not the problem. For Serbians, speaking French was. We were so naïve in thinking that, if we had studied French, so would have any Serbian in Yugoslavia.

We couldn't communicate with this man. Ollie and I began speaking in Romanian to each other about our next move.

The man smiled and said in Romanian, "You are Romanians?"

The northeastern part of Serbia, called Vojvodina, contains a part of Banat, the region we came from; the larger part of Banat is in Romania. In this area there are many ethnic groups, including Romanians, just as there are Serbians in the Romanian Banat. Ollie's uncle and family, here in Vojvodina, were ethnic Romanians, and so was this man we happened to meet there.

After we recovered from our shock, we spoke with him. We told him that we had escaped from Romania and were trying to go to the West. He said that from time to time he had seen others just like us. We asked him which way to go to find Alibunar, and he told us to take the left branch of the highway. He wished us good luck, we thanked him, and we continued on our blistery feet and aching legs toward our destination.

After a while, Ollie turned around and said, "That guy is coming after us with two big dogs."

This was trouble we didn't need. The man was riding a bicycle toward us, escorted by two mutts. I figured he decided to stop us and make a citizen's arrest or something like that. I reached in my bag and grabbed my knife. With my thumb I unsheathed the knife, but I didn't take it out of the bag. I was determined that I would not give up without a fight. Never before had I carried a knife nor pulled a knife on anyone, as I was about to do now. But this was a matter of life and death. I was not going to give up easily.

The two of us stood in the road with pale faces, waiting for the man to catch up with us. I was more concerned about the dogs than I was about him, and I wondered how I could fight them. When he got near us he stopped, got off the bike, and the dogs came over to sniff us.

To our surprise he pulled out a bill of Yugoslavian dinars and offered it to us. He then told us, "It is a long way to walk to Alibunar, but you can buy tickets and take the bus, which will stop near that town." He even took us to the nearby bus stop on the highway and wished us good luck. We thanked him again, amazed at this goodwill gesture.

It is incredible how generous people can be when they see someone in need. This Romanian-Yugoslavian, whose name we never found out, helped us for no other reason than pity for us. We looked at each other and then watched him disappear into the distance, going home followed by his dogs. We couldn't comprehend what we had done to deserve this act of kindness.

The bus came; we paid for our tickets and asked the driver for Alibunar. He nodded in acknowledgement, and we sat down, relieved to take a load off our feet. I would guess that the distance the bus took us would have taken us another two days by foot. At one stop, the driver said, "Alibunar," pointing toward a nearby road. We got off, closer to our destination.

We began to walk stiffly in the direction the driver had pointed out. As we were walking on the road, a horse wagon came alongside us. We asked, "Alibunar?" and the old man in the wagon motioned to us to get in his wagon. The man was not Romanian, but Ollie mentioned his uncle's name, and the man seemed to know him. We reached Alibunar, where the old man delivered us to the front gate of Ollie's uncle's house.

16. OLLIE'S UNCLE

We knocked at the gate and an older man answered. Baffled, he stared at us. We probably looked like two dirty, tired, and hungry dogs, no different from two escapees from a concentration camp, minus the striped clothes. His eyes nearly jumped out of his head when he recognized Ollie. He invited us in, peering around outside to see if any of the neighbors or passersby had noticed our arrival. The street was deserted. Once behind the gate, he and Ollie hugged, and then Ollie introduced me to him and to the rest of the family.

After he poured us each a shot of plum brandy – for medicinal purposes – we told him what had happened and how we had arrived at his house. He was happy that we had made it, but worried about the next leg of our trip. We weren't sure which country to go to: Italy or Austria. We found out from him that Austria's border was mountainous and difficult to cross because of its terrain. Italy's border was easier. So we decided to go to Italy. But before starting again we needed to rest.

Dinner was served: Beef-and-green-bean stew in tomato sauce! Ollie and I couldn't believe our eyes. It was just what we had wished to eat when we were talking about food earlier. We were terribly hungry. Ollie and I each had three helpings. After dinner, Ollie's uncle showed us to our room, and we slept for over twelve hours.

The next day, we began to tend to our wounds. We had blisters on the bottoms of our feet the size of sand dollars. Some of mine had broken earlier, and they were excruciatingly painful. Our legs ached, and we walked like two old men. We stayed at Ollie's uncle's house for several days, recovering from our ordeal. One day, to show my appreciation, I cooked crepes for the family, a specialty that my dad had taught me when I was a kid. I guess I impressed the family with my ability to flip them in the air, and the good-tasting crepes stuffed with apricot marmalade got me thinking that things were looking up.

***

A few days later, Ollie's uncle sent a cousin of his to visit Ollie's parents in Timisoara. Phoning them was out of the question; I don't think Ollie's parents had a phone (privates phone were a rarity during those times), and, if they did, their phone would have been monitored by the secret police.

Yugoslavian citizens had a lot more freedom to travel abroad than Romanians did. The cousin had a passport, so she was able to go to Romania. She carried a letter from Ollie's uncle that was sewn into the hem of her dress. That was a good precaution, considering that she had to go through Romanian customs, which did not leave the smallest detail, including pockets, unchecked. At least my parents and Ollie's parents would know that we were safe and that we would attempt to cross the border into Italy.

17. TO ITALY

By Friday we were in much better shape and ready to continue our journey. On Saturday morning we said our good-byes to Ollie's relatives and, accompanied by Ollie's uncle, we traveled to Belgrade, the Yugoslavian capital. The plan was to take the overnight train to Trieste, Italy; before the border we would get off and make it on foot across the border, just as we had in Romania. Ollie's uncle bought us two train tickets and took us to the platform where the train would depart. I remember the three of us eating vanilla ice cream just before boarding the train.

On the train we searched for an empty compartment so we wouldn't have to converse with anyone and be discovered as refugees. We found a compartment where only a little old lady sat. We joined her, smiling and nodding after she greeted us, and the train left the station. Soon it was dark, and we tried to catch some shut-eye. As we were napping, the door to the compartment suddenly opened and two guys peered inside, checking the overhead baggage racks. They left, but it felt like something was not right.

Ollie stepped out into the corridor for a smoke. A minute later he came in and said, "Those two guys we saw earlier are coming down the corridor with a cop. They're checking every compartment."

This was trouble. It seemed that someone's baggage had been stolen and they were looking for it. I looked at the little old lady who was sleeping in her seat and told Ollie, "Pretend to sleep – this way we won't have to answer any questions."

The compartment's door flew open and the cop came in with the other two men behind him. I pretended to sleep, but had my eyes open a slit to see through my eyelashes. The cop looked at the three of us; at the rack above us, which was empty; and at the rack above the old lady, which had her luggage. Then, without waking us, he and the other two left. It seems that an old lady and two teenagers looked harmless – perhaps just a grandmother with her two grandsons traveling at night, he may have thought.

The rest of the trip was uneventful, with Ollie spending a lot of time out in the corridor, smoking and watching. I remember the train stopping in Ljubljana, the capital of Slovenia and the last major city in Yugoslavia, after which we began moving faster toward the Italian border. Dawn approached, and we were able to see outside.

Ollie came in from the corridor all agitated. "Cops!"

"What now?" I asked.

"I think they're checking IDs," said Ollie.

It was the same drill all over again: Before the border station, the cops were checking either IDs or passports since this train would cross into Italy. Time to put some distance between us and the cops. We walked toward the end of the train. We even opened an outside door to check if we could jump out, but this train was moving too fast, at least sixty miles per hour, unlike the train we rode back in Romania. Things were getting uncomfortable as we reached the last car. We considered getting

99

outside and hanging low onto the steps of the train to avoid capture.

The train stopped – not at a station, but in the middle of nowhere in the woods. It stopped for a red light, waiting for another train to pass in the opposite direction. This was all we needed. We jumped off the train, descending the steep embankment of the railroad tracks. After a short walk through woods and pastures we found a road that seemed to parallel the railroad tracks. We took that road, checking from time to time that it was going in the same direction as the railroad.

Eventually, the road diverged from the railroad's direction, but it kept heading west. It was an unpaved gravel road, not frequented by many vehicles. We found it curious that the kilometer markers were written in Italian. Were we in Italy already? But when did we cross the border? Did the train cross the border before we jumped off? But the police had seemed to be Yugoslavian, not Italian. These were questions we couldn't answer, but we kept pressing ahead. What we didn't know at that time was that this area was part of Italy once, but now it was Yugoslavia, and the kilometer stones dated from the Italian times. It did add to our confusion about our whereabouts.

Someplace along the road we met a young man and asked him if this road was going to Trieste. There was not much conversation between us, more like us saying "Trieste?" and pointing to the road and then pointing in a westerly direction. He said something and then nodded, affirming our assumption. He asked us, by some mutually understood words and signs, where we were from. We said, "Romania." We pointed to the west and asked "Italia?" He understood what we were up to. He shook his head and said something we didn't understand. He then put his wrists together as if in handcuffs. Somehow we understood that if we got to Italy, we would be arrested and returned back.

That was terrible news. I thought that once we were in Italy we could ask for political asylum and that then we would be free. What was going on? We must have looked scared, because the man somehow explained that we should not ask for asylum in Trieste, but that we should go farther into Italy and then ask for asylum. We thanked him and parted company.

We walked all day through a beautiful, hilly landscape until the road we were on turned into a paved road again and joined with a larger highway, which headed straight west. It was the right highway leading to the Italian border; we could see signs with information about the international border. In the late afternoon we stopped at a roadside restaurant to have dinner. Ollie's uncle had given us money for food, and we sure needed it. Both of us had a schnitzel steak and fried potatoes. We had beer, too, but perhaps too much, because I got a buzz.

Feeling satisfied and more courageous because of the beer, we approached the Yugoslavian-Italian border. Many cars were heading toward the border or coming from it. It was not completely dark, but we could see the bright lights marking the border crossing. There was no way we could just walk to the border and run across it. The Yugoslavian border was a communist border and was guarded as such, although we didn't see any watchtowers like the ones we had seen in Romania.

18. NEAR THE ITALIAN BORDER

In spite of our long trek on the highway, we hadn't been stopped by the police or border patrols even as we were getting very close to the border zone. A similar spot at the Romanian border would have been buzzing with border patrols. The best way to get across this border, we figured, was to circumvent the border crossing and customs. For some reason we decided to bypass customs on the left side, a path that ascended into the hills. We crossed the highway and walked away from the lights through pastures and rocky terrain and occasional clumps of bushes and trees. At the place we deemed far enough away, where we couldn't hear the traffic but could see the bright lights of the border crossing, we made a right turn and headed for the border.

We began walking in a crouched position, running from bush to bush and from tree to tree. We stopped often to listen for border patrols. It was all quiet and getting darker. Unlike the Romanian border where the terrain was flat, here it was hilly, rough, and full of rocks. We passed by some old fence posts that might have been left there from some old fence before entering a grove of trees.

We walked through the small grove until we came to the edge of a flat, long, and wide pasture. That was too much of an open area; we couldn't risk crossing it without being spotted. What worked once could work again, so we decided to camp there under the trees and the next day, at the crack of dawn, we would attempt to cross the pasture and the border beyond it.

It was early next morning when we woke up. I didn't check my watch this time, and there was no need to strike a match. It was light enough, and I could see what I hadn't seen when we arrived at that spot the night before. To our horror, what appeared to be a pasture last night was, this morning, a long and wide chasm, dropping down a hundred feet or more. In the dark last night, the tops of the trees growing at the bottom had given us the impression of grass. We could have easily stepped to our deaths the evening before. We had actually slept near the edge of the drop.

We found a way down partly around the chasm, partly through it, and eventually we ended up in another area of pastures, with patches of trees and fieldstone walls serving as fences. We ran from growth to growth, taking cover and advancing, until we heard dogs barking. They were slightly to our right, there were many of them, and they were coming toward us, barking and growling. Those must have been the border patrol dogs. They had heard us and they were coming for blood. We turned and ran as fast as we could. We jumped and climbed over fieldstone wall after fieldstone wall, some as tall we were, but that didn't slow us down. Panic and fear turbocharged us for a while. We ran until we couldn't run anymore.

Bent over and breathing heavily, we stopped and wondered how soon the dogs, followed by the border patrols, would catch up with us. But there was no onslaught of vicious German Shepherds or mean border patrols. We could hardly hear the dogs any more. Could we have lost them? We had jumped over a lot of walls. We decided not to linger and continued walking in the right direction, figuring that it was the way across the border.

It was pre-dawn now. Light fog floated above the pastures. We continued running from bush to bush in search of the border. We climbed across an embankment and discovered a highway at the top. This was a surprise. What road was this? One that continued to the border crossing, or was it some other road in Yugoslavia? We were lost. Again.

However, something was different about this road. For one thing, it was wider. I bent down and touched the asphalt. It was coarse and gray. The asphalt on the roads I knew from Romania and Yugoslavia were black and smooth, not like this one. Along the highway we spotted billboards. We'd never seen advertising billboards before. The ads on them were written in Italian. We could read and understand most of the words because Romanian and Italian are similar. Could those be pre-border advertisements? Where could we be?

No time to waste. We had to push on. We walked along the highway as the sun rose behind us. At least we were walking in the right direction, judging by the sun. The walk was easy because the highway was going downhill. We gawked at the billboards, not understanding why there were so many of them. How many times do you have to advertise for this Campari drink? Occasionally a car passed by, and each one was an Italian car, not the usual forest green trucks we had seen in Yugoslavia. We kept walking.

We came around a turn and, lo and behold, down below us we saw the Adriatic Sea. I'd never seen the sea in my life. It was vast, a purple-blue in color, and I felt as if it were sucking me toward it. I had a moment of vertigo, but I quickly recovered and took in the unbelievable site. At the bottom, on the shore, was a big city. Without mistake, that was Trieste.

We were in Italy. How and when we crossed the border, we had no idea. A feeling of elation engulfed us. We made it! Did we make it? Yes, we did!

We were free, free, free! We hugged and danced with joy. We had gotten out of hell!

Now what would we do?

It took us a few more hours, but we finally entered the city. Trieste was just like we imagined an Italian city would be from watching TV and movies. We were walking with our eyes wide and mouths open, staring at this new environment. It was as if we were in an alien, extraterrestrial city. It was so different from what we were used to. We continued down the streets until we arrived in a square, or piazza.

Ollie and I conferred on what to do next. Should we go farther? The next big city would be Venice. We had no idea how to get out of Trieste or how to find the road to Venice. And we were tired. That man back in Yugoslavia didn't know what he was talking about when he told us that we would be turned back. Both of us had heard in Romania and from Ollie's uncle that once we were in Italy we were free. We talked each other into asking for political asylum from the police.

We looked around the piazza and saw someone who resembled a policeman. He looked more like a locomotive conductor back in Romania, but he was the only uniformed man in the square, dressed in a dark blue uniform with golden trim. We approached him with trepidation. Ollie's sister back in Romania had an Italian boyfriend who visited them from time to time, so Ollie spoke some Italian. I, along with him, could understand it fairly well.

Ollie asked for political asylum. The policeman looked at us and he seemed to know at once who or what we were. I had a feeling that this was not the first time he had seen our kind, escapees from behind the Iron Curtain. He asked us if we wanted asylum in Italy. We were confused; we wanted to

105

immigrate to America or Canada, not Italy. We did not want to offend him by choosing another country over Italy, so we accepted what he said, reluctantly. The policeman asked the right question, but we didn't know the difference between asylum and immigration.

He blew his whistle and a police minivan stopped near us. The police driver asked us to get in and, a few streets later, we arrived at the police station. They had us wait in a room until a plainclothes detective came in and asked for our IDs. It seemed that this all was a fairly routine business around here. He looked kind of bored and unenthusiastic about processing us. Or maybe it was because it was Monday morning, and he had the Monday morning blues. Too much Campari? Hard to say. He booked us, meaning he wrote our names in a roster, after which he opened the door and took us to another police minivan.

Once we were seated, the van took off to some unknown destination. But soon after, horror struck us. The van was going back on the same road we had arrived on – it was taking us back to the border! That man in Yugoslavia had told us the truth. We were not free, we were arrested, and we were about to be deported. I exchanged glances with Ollie. Both of us were livid. We made it to Italy in one piece only to be returned back to Romania? I debated what to do. Pull my knife on the cops? Not a chance. I was so scared and nervous that I couldn't tell which end of the knife was the right end. Jump out of the van and run? Maybe.

Just as I was considering such an option, the van veered from the main highway onto a side road. This was a new road, not the one we came by. Maybe it was a back road to the border? Ollie and I were looking out through the windows with anguish and dread. We had no idea what was going on.

The van arrived in front of a tall, gated, chain-link fence with barbed wire on top. The gate opened and let us inside a compound. I had heard that in Italy and other free countries the people who managed to escape communism were taken to refugee camps. This must have been a refugee camp. The van door opened, and we were taken to a two-story building, where we were placed in a large room with jail bars on it. I remember vividly the sound of the door slamming shut behind us.

In the room a few dozen men stared at us. All at once, they started asking us in Hungarian, Czech, Albanian, Polish, Bulgarian, Russian, and Romanian about our nationality. "We are Romanians," we answered.

The non-Romanians returned to the double-stacked cots that lined the walls. The Romanian men approached us. We were kids compared to them. They were all in their thirties to sixties.

"Welcome. You are safe. Don't worry," said one of them.

"Why are we in jail?" I asked.

"We are all newcomers. We got here a couple of days ago, and they need to process us. Italians don't work on Saturdays and Sundays."

They don't work on Saturday? Everyone works six days a week back in Romania. We were told that in capitalist countries the business owners worked people to death. Another lie.

"You're lucky you got here today. Some of us have been here since Friday. You'll be processed along with us and released in the camp in a few hours."

"Where are we?" I asked.

"In the refugee camp in Padriciano. How did you get out of Romania?" The men were burning with curiosity.

"We escaped," said Ollie.

"We crossed the border," I added. They shook their heads in disbelief, seeing how young we were.

"Where in Romania are you from?"

"Timisoara," I answered. Most of them were from Bucharest, the Romanian capital.

"How old are you?" asked another.

"Eighteen," Ollie told them. We stood close together, not yet recovered from our scare.

"Jesus," they murmured.

"So young, and you got across illegally?" wondered another. We nodded.

"Don't be afraid. You are free and safe," added another one, who noticed our fear.

We finally exhaled. We were free and sheltered, although behind bars. Later we found out that we were the youngest among all the Romanian refugees at that time, with the exception of the children of families that managed to escape together. At least in this group we were the only ones who had gotten out illegally from Romania. These men had defected while on vacation in Italy or in other countries. There were women, too, but in another wing, separated from the men.

From time to time, Romania allowed a man or a woman, but rarely a couple, to visit a Western country like Italy. If they were single, young, and non-communist party members, their chances of exiting Romania on a tourist visa were slim. Only married people and only one of the couple could do so. The other spouse was kept back in Romania to assure that the traveling spouse would not defect. But they often defected in spite of being separated from their families. Being free was worth the sacrifice of leaving their loved ones for many years.

19. LIFE AS A REFUGEE IN ITALY

That same day, we were processed and given refugee IDs. The camp's staff gave us blankets and toiletries, and we were assigned beds in common rooms. We were given vouchers to buy clothes in Trieste later. I bought my first pair of blue jeans at that time.

The men were kept separate from the women, but the couples and families were allowed to stay together. We were fed three meals a day, but had nothing to do but wait to be taken to one of two other refugee camps in Italy for immigration to other countries.

We stayed in the Padriciano camp for a month. We could leave the camp during the day, and Ollie and I ventured into Trieste to see this new world. I felt that I was born anew. There was so much different and unusual stuff around there. One day we saw small buns in a bakery; they were so perfect, rosy and shiny. We thought they were made of porcelain until we saw someone take a bite out of one. It was bread; we had never seen bread like that before.

We saw produce that we thought was made of wax, for display. But they were real: shiny green bell peppers, translucent-skinned potatoes, plump tomatoes, and crisp and shimmering cabbage. Those were in contrast to the dirty and broken bell peppers, dirt-encrusted potatoes, smashed tomatoes, and elephant-trampled cabbage that we knew back home. And the people were able to select the vegetables and fruits they wanted, as many as they wanted, and not have them just dumped in a limited quantity into their bags. There were no lines anywhere, not even at the butcher shop. There was plenty of

110

meat of all kinds. We had been told that people in the West were starving. It was hard to believe the lies anymore, seeing all this abundance. Those communist bastards!

There were cars everywhere. We'd never seen so many cars before. And the Italians seemed happy, enjoying cappuccinos and gelati in outdoor cafes. We had been told that the West was poor and suffering, and that people were unemployed and not able to afford the bare necessities; if it hadn't been for the food that Romania exported to them, the West would have starved. Lies, lies, and more lies – the communists had told us lie after lie while destroying our souls.

The Padriciano refugee camp was within sight of the Italian-Yugoslavian border. We could see it on top of the hill nearby. When we escaped, we crossed the Yugoslavian border without knowing it, and we had actually slept in Italy. The fence posts that we thought belonged to an old fence were the border demarcations. The dogs that we thought were chasing us were Italian dogs, probably belonging to an Italian farmer. As far as being deported from Italy, as that man in Yugoslavia had told us, he was referring to the fate of some Yugoslavians. Unlike Romanians, Yugoslavians were free to travel to the West, but, for whatever reason, some were turned back when they asked for political asylum.

Ollie and I had to get the border-fear-monkey off our backs, so one day we hiked to the border near the camp. There were no watchtowers, no barbed wire fences, and no strip of land to detect who had crossed the border at night. There were no border patrols, either. Six-foot tall, four-by-four black-and-white-painted posts marked the border. What a contrast between the communist Romanian border and a Western border. (Yugoslavia was communist mostly in name.)

While there, we had to do one more thing: cross the border back into Yugoslavia. Although it was obvious that there was no threat, we stepped across the invisible line with fear and trepidation. It was like being in the ocean and swimming from the shallow water over the deepest oceanic chasm. It felt as if Yugoslavian border patrols were waiting to grab us and ship our butts back to Romania. We stayed in Yugoslavia for a fraction of a second and then ran back into Italy. What a relief to be on safe ground again! The fear of what we had left behind us was so deep, that even stepping back across an imaginary line, back into communism, gave us chills.

While in the camp I met many other refugees. A large percentage of Romanians got out while on vacation in Italy or other countries. Most were alone, their spouses and children kept behind in Romania as a deterrent against asking for political asylum while in a free country. Complete families were not allowed to travel to Western countries unless they were trusted communist members. But even trusted communists defected. Other families were allowed to visit a communist sister country such as Hungary. Cleverly, these families, while in the Hungarian capital of Budapest, would go to the Italian embassy and asked for tourist visas. Once armed with visas, they would take the train to Italy. Hungarian customs would not realize that the visas had been issued in Hungary, not Romania, and so would let them through.

The majority of the refugees without families, mostly men, were professionals and communist party members. For a professional in communist Romania to be promoted, becoming a communist party member was mandatory. A handful of these individuals were allowed to visit Italy and a few other Western countries to give the impression that Romanians, too, could travel abroad, although their families were kept behind to ensure there were no defections. Most of these tourists were screened and investigated thoroughly to ensure that their motives were tourism, not defection, before they were given exit visas – yes, that is correct, an *exit visa*. If you are an American and you travel abroad, have you ever gotten an exit visa from the State Department? Of course not, not in a free country.

A lot of these Romanian Western-culture-seeking tourists wanted to travel to a free country to defect, to get out of hell, even if it meant leaving behind their spouses and kids. The hope was that once established in the West, they would be able to bring their families to the new country. Most of the time it worked, but only after many, many years of red tape and a substantial amount of money. Sometimes, some of these men had to go on hunger strikes in front of the UN to bring to the media's attention communist Romania's refusal to release their families. Nicolae Ceausescu, the Romanian Fuhrer, was delighted to burnish his reputation in the West as a maverick – he wanted to be seen as bucking the will of the Soviet Union. Because he didn't want his reputation tarnished, these hunger strikes usually led to the release of the defectors' families.

I thought that once a Romanian arrived in a free country, defecting would be as easy as pie. Compared with what Ollie and I, and many others like us, had had to endure to get to Italy, being taken to Italy on vacation was a deluxe form of escape. It may have been deluxe, but it was no less traumatic. The excursions originated from Romania by bus. The bus driver, a tourist guide, and a travel security guard escorted the tourists to protect them from "criminal elements" in the West. The three official employees of the tourist company were really secret police agents. There were additional secret police agents, traveling incognito, pretending to be tourists. Their jobs were to find out who was planning to defect and to use psychological pressure, or even threats against their loved ones back in Romania, to stop them from defecting. In spite of their diligence, constant presence, chaperoning, and subtle intimidation, there were defections. But the defectors did not consider what they did an easy task.

Most Romanians were imprisoned in their own minds. I was. The biggest fear for me was not risking my life in the act of border crossing, but the actual act of defecting. There was a fear, a mental Berlin Wall that was not to be crossed. It was as if the long arm of the secret police had an invisible chain around my neck. And all other defectors felt the same way. One Romanian tourist defector told me that there were ten others on his bus who wanted to defect, but sheer terror kept them in their seats, and they returned home.

The fear of the secret police's presence, even in the West, was not totally unfounded. From time to time, we would hear on Radio Free Europe that certain dissidents residing in the West had been assassinated. In the Padriciano camp, there was a Romanian defector who raised the suspicions of his more astute countrymen. This fellow was very inquisitive about everyone, even visiting the men's dormitories, as if inspecting the premises. His police/military mannerisms gave him away. I saw him, but I was too young to know the difference, however, the more seasoned men spotted him and told everyone to be aware of this guy; he could be a secret police agent sent to investigate those who had defected. A few days later, this fellow was gone. We guessed that he had fulfilled his investigation and returned back to Romania to report what he had found.

I befriended many tourist defectors, and I heard their stories. Exchanging escape stories was common. In one case, three people, a couple and a man, defected together. The couple were in their fifties, communist party members, and, because they were older, they were considered a good risk to allow to travel together to Italy. (This older, childless couple was not considered an asset for the state; if they were to defect, communist Romania would have two less retired people to take care of.) The other man, Jim, who later became a good friend of mine, was a communist party member as well. His family was left behind in Romania.

As it happened, the three of them discovered their common goal: defection. They conspired and planned their escape from a hotel in Italy. It was not as if they were locked in their rooms at night, but fear kept many inside. These three agreed that, after the travel security guard – in reality a secret police agent – made his final rounds, knocking on each tourist's door around ten o'clock to make sure everyone was "OK," they would leave the hotel to ask for political asylum.

An hour after the final check, and making sure all was quiet outside in the corridor, the three of them snuck out of their rooms, carrying their luggage, and quietly tiptoed to the elevator. They prayed that when the door opened they wouldn't find the secret police inside. They didn't. They descended to the lobby, peering around the elevator door to see if the coast was clear. It was.

And then they made a mad dash for the exit. Jim held his luggage in front of him like a shield, intent on knocking down the ever-vigilant secret police agent, as they busted through the door onto the street. The street was empty.

The three of them ran, luggage in hand, for several blocks until they were exhausted, hoping that they had put enough distance between themselves and the hotel. The woman had been a track and field athlete in her youth and later she said that, that night, she ran the best four hundred meters of her life. And she finished first, holding onto her luggage, ahead of Jim and her older husband, who was panting as if he were about to have a heart attack.

115

There was no way for the secret police agent to prevent them from leaving, but that was not what they thought. Others were not so daring as to leave from their hotel rooms at night or in the morning. Instead, they "got lost" in the crowds as they were visiting a point of interest or tourist site. They gladly left their luggage behind, just to get away unharmed.

While in the camp, I mingled with Poles, Bulgarians, Czechoslovakians, and Hungarians, especially one Hungarian who happened to be a cute girl. I learned about other people's lives and how they managed to get out of their respective countries. Romania and Poland were the only communist countries that were surrounded by other communist countries. East Germany bordered on West Germany, but that was where the infamous Berlin Wall stood. Czechoslovakia and Hungary had borders with Austria. Bulgaria had borders with Turkey and Greece. Those borders must have been pure hell to cross, as many citizens of those countries ended up escaping through Yugoslavia, and then to Italy or Austria. One Bulgarian fellow showed us his wrists, broken when he was forced to jump from a second story by the police. Another Bulgarian of Turkish ancestry told us how he had been tortured by the Bulgarian secret police, who had applied electrical charges to his testicles.

We met a refugee from Spain. Unlike the rest of us fleeing from communism, this fellow was getting out of fascist Spain. Franco was for him what Ceausescu was for Romanians. A group of Romanians, me included, befriended him, sharing a common Romance language (after Italian, Spanish is the second closest language to Romanian.) We were amazed that he wanted to get out of Spain. And, to our astonishment, he wished to immigrate to the Soviet Union. He was a communist, for sure, and no matter what we told him about communism, it did not dissuade him. I guess one person's hell is another's paradise. We could only imagine what his shock would be like after living in the Soviet Union even for a brief period of time. But then, who knows?

What he may not have known was that once in the Soviet Union, and after he was integrated into Soviet society, he would not be allowed to leave that country. He would become another slave in the communist empire. I hope he did OK.

Many other Romanian refugees who had escaped illegally like us told us their horror stories of being caught, beaten, and incarcerated for years when they had previously tried to escape. Most of these fellows had missing teeth from the beatings they had received while in custody. In spite of the brutal treatment and imprisonment, these fellows did not give up and tried escaping again and again until they made it to freedom.

A few people managed to escape across the Danube. I met a fellow who swam across at night and almost died of hypothermia after swimming for more than an hour. I had a good friend who crossed the river in an inflatable boat the size of an inner tube. Even in a boat paddling across the river, it took him over a half hour to reach the other shore. An inflatable rowboat is no match for a high-speed border patrol boat, but that night my friend was lucky; he made it across safely. The patrols must have been preoccupied with other matters.

One defector was a former border patrol guard. This fellow could not dare escape while he was a soldier on border duty, because had he been caught, he would have been executed. He waited until he was discharged from the military before escaping. He told me about the flares Ollie and I had seen when we crossed the Romanian border. Red flares meant that the border patrol had caught some people trying to escape. I asked about the shots we heard. He commented that the border patrols were allowed to shoot into the air as a warning not to flee. I hope he was right and that no one was killed.

After a month in the Padriciano camp, some of us were transferred to another camp in Latina, near Rome, to start the immigration process. Here is where I spent most of my time in Italy, and during that time I had a chance to observe life in a free country. I witnessed a rally of local fascists in a piazza and listened to their political speeches. I had thought that the fascists had been eradicated, but here they were.

To my consternation, I witnessed an even bigger rally by the Italian Communist Party. I had risked my life to get out of a communist hell and here these Italians, plump and happy, who never had to stand in line for their daily bread, were striving to bring communism to Italy. Go figure. This communist rally was peppered with red flags carrying the yellow insignia of the hammer and sickle. The communist flag to me was as hideous as the Nazi flag. Even today, the red communist flag reminds me of the psychological torture communists are able to inflict on people.

I wanted to immigrate to the United States, but the Vietnam War gave me pause. I wasn't afraid of being drafted into the military and sent to Vietnam (after all, I felt I was bulletproof). I was afraid of being captured in Vietnam by the Vietcong, taken to North Vietnam, and shipped to the Romanian Embassy, where some communist comrade with rotten teeth would grin at me and say, "Comrade Sandru, we've been waiting for you. We're going to ship you back to Romania and throw your ass into the deepest and darkest jail. For life!" It might sound funny now, but that was what I feared the most.

I applied to immigrate to Canada instead. Ollie had relatives in Canada, so his prospects of being sponsored were much better than mine. But Canada was choosy; it didn't want a runaway high school dropout like me. Even Ollie, with relatives residing there, was rejected. Too bad for Canada.

For us, the USA was meant to be. Both Ollie and I applied, and America said yes. America saw the potential in us, and, by God, I wasn't going to disappoint her, or something like that. Ten months after we had arrived in Italy, I immigrated to the United States, taking the plane to New York. Ollie went to Detroit at a later date.

The author in front of Coliseum, Rome, before departing to America

While I was in Italy, in Latina, I rolled up my sleeves and did whatever odd jobs I could find: working in the vineyards, picking up watermelons, digging, carrying, loading, and construction work. I even found a permanent job working in a hardware and metal distributor as a yard hand. I worked hard, earned money, bought things like clothes and even a guitar that

I couldn't have hoped to obtain in Romania. I even saved a small amount of money, which served me well later in the US.

20. IN RETROSPECT

Ollie and I were two dumb, lucky kids. We made it out through the eye of a needle. I chose the spot to cross the border without ever having seen the border before that time. The section of the border we crossed was sparsely populated and heavily used for agriculture, which made it impractical for the border patrols to fence or wire with tripflares. There were plenty of deep ditches, though.

We were lucky – by twenty minutes – not to be in front of the horseback-patrolling soldier. We could have been scooped up before even getting near the border. We were lucky to find haystacks for shelter after we were drenched in the storm in the middle of nowhere.

We were very lucky that some other people attempted to cross the border in our vicinity; unfortunately for them, they were caught. I hope they were not killed. Their capture distracted the border patrols enough for us to slip through. On the night we spent under the watchtower, the border was patrolled within a dozen yards from where we were. That night, the patrol may have fallen asleep, and we crossed the border unharmed.

We were lucky that the Yugoslavian police did not catch us, and that a Good Samaritan gave us money for bus fare to reach Alibunar. I, at least, was very lucky to partner with Ollie, who had relatives in Yugoslavia, who helped us with the train fare to travel to the Italian border. We were even luckier not to be bitten by the dogs, although they were Italian dogs and perhaps less vicious than communist dogs.

We didn't suffer the fate of many others who didn't make it or who made it only after many attempts, hardships, torture, and prison.

We were lucky.

And, of course, we were lucky that the USA accepted us as immigrants to America.

God bless America!

21. AMERICA, AMERICA

In late April of 1972, I arrived at New York's John F. Kennedy airport. I was free, and I had arrived in the Promised Land. I felt like Stavros in the movie *America, America* by Elia Kazan, finally making it to the land of dreams. I saw New York's skyline from the taxi taking me to Manhattan. I remember having seen it occasionally in movies, but in real life it was impressive. The Empire State Building was illuminated, resembling a gothic church spire shooting into the sky. "New York City, here I come!" I thought excitedly.

I had left Romania with just the shirt on my back and arrived ten months later in America with $100 and a few belongings that I had acquired while working in Italy. The Romanian Orthodox Church sponsored me and, besides the airplane ticket to New York, they gave me $20 and one-week's paid hotel room in Manhattan, for which I was very thankful.

I was on my own from that point on, and no other aid was available after that. In Romania I had lived a sheltered life, and in the refugee camps in Italy I had had room and board, but now, in New York, I was on my own. It was sink or swim, and I swam. I barely spoke English, and I had no skills, but I was willing to work.

Friends I had made in Italy came over to the hotel and helped me move in with my friend Jim to share his apartment. It was better than the hotel, and it cut down on expenses for both Jim and me.

In America everything was so big. The buildings were tall, the streets were wide, and the cars were huge. Even the stove and refrigerator in our apartment were big. America was big, and that was reflected in all aspects of life. The skyscrapers were indeed scraping the sky, and the view from the top of the Empire State Building was incredible. I could see the twin towers of the World Trade Center, which in 1972 were under construction. Farther in the distance I could see the Statue of Liberty.

Soon after, I went to visit the famous statue. I bought my ticket and left to get on the boat, when the ticket salesman shouted after me. "What was wrong?" I thought. I had given him a $20 bill, but I had neglected to take my change back. The man insisted I come back and get my change. I was dumbfounded; he could have pocketed the money, and no one would have been the wiser. That was my first experience with the honesty that prevails in America, which I encountered many times afterward.

As the boat got closer to the Statue of Liberty, I became overwhelmed by its size and what it symbolized. I had seen Lady Liberty before in a movie, *Saboteur*, but now here I was seeing it in its full blue-green splendor. Wow! I had to climb up to the viewing deck in the statue's head, and, by God, I was there just as I had seen it in the movie. Sadly, I couldn't find the stairway that led up the arm to the torch.

The author and the Statue of Liberty

I worked hard; sometimes I even held two full-time jobs. The manual work I was doing in the beginning was OK for a start and to make a living, but it wasn't my life's desire. My parents raised me to believe in education. The question was not if I would go to university, but rather which major I should choose. There was a problem, though: I did not finish my high school education. In reality, I was a high school dropout. In the fall of 1972, I enrolled in night classes for my high school diploma. It was disheartening to find out that it would take me four years to finish my last year of high school at night, while working to support myself.

Fortunately, in school they had problems placing me in some courses, especially in mathematics and the sciences. I was too advanced in many subjects. The high school administration recommended that I take the New York State High School Equivalency Diploma examination, the GED. I did so, and I passed. I had obtained my high school diploma practically overnight. May I say, "What a country!" There was more than one path to achieve my dreams. I could now enroll in college.

I continued taking classes in English and grammar at that high school, and one evening I met a cute girl of Armenian descent from Romania. I found out from her that she worked as a draftsperson in a company that hired "fresh off the boat" immigrants. I have a talent for drawing, and I had taken a course or two in technical drafting back in high school, so it sounded like work I would enjoy doing. Without delay I applied for a job at that company, and I was hired. Now I was a draftsman. I had steady and full-time employment. It paid minimum hourly wages, $1.95 per hour, but every three months I would get a nickel raise as I got better at my job. Being good in sciences and math, and working as a technical draftsman, I realized that a career in engineering was what I would be good at and would like to pursue.

I had received a temporary green card as an immigrant and resident, but I didn't think that was proper identification, so I asked a colleague at work where I could get an ID. In Romania, the identification document resembled a passport. He laughed and said, "ID? What for? I'm a free man, not a dog that needs an ID." After I got my American citizenship, I didn't have even a card to serve as an ID, except for my driver's license. Free men and women don't have IDs. What a concept!

The political freedom in the US was astonishing. In a shop window I saw a poster of Richard Nixon. Very disrespectful, I thought: He was sitting on the toilet with his pants around his ankles and his tie hanging between his knees, hiding his private parts. After I had stared at it for a while, I looked nervously over my shoulder, expecting at any moment to be snatched by the secret police for viewing the politically defaming poster. Old fears die hard. In the US, the president serves the people; he doesn't own the people, like Ceausescu did in Romania.

I had never read the Constitution of the United States or the Bill of Rights until I came to America. The first time I read the Bill of Rights I was dumbfounded, because, somehow, I already knew it. But I had never read it before. What happened is that the Founding Fathers had written those pages based on the natural instincts of every human on Earth. God created each one of us hardwired with the Constitution in our minds and souls. The Constitution of the United States of America felt natural; it felt as if it were written for me, as an individual, and not for the communist party.

The first amendment guarantees religious freedom, free speech, and freedom of the press (without a zillion exceptions or guidelines of what constitutes free speech). Also, it provides for the right to assemble, meaning to demonstrate, which was a crime in communist Romania. The second amendment calls for the right to bear arms, arms that a citizen can use to defend against a despotic government. Interesting!

The fourth amendment covers search and seizure; the police cannot search you on a whim. And the rest of the amendments were all designed for one's freedom and safety from the government. In communist Romania, the police were to be feared. It was imprudent to be near them, and, if you had to talk to them, they treated you like a second-class citizen. The New York cops were jovial, easy-going, and respectful. There was nothing to fear from them, unless you were a criminal.

Brilliant! That's why America is America.

I realized why I was so at odds with communism. Sure, communist Romania had a constitution, but, unlike the American Constitution, the communist constitution was full of exceptions, guidelines, prohibitions, and examples of what is politically correct. The constitution was not written for the individual, but for the communist party.

Within a few short years, because we were living in different parts of the US, I lost track of Ollie. I hope he's doing well, wherever he is nowadays. Our life paths overlapped for a brief period of time, but that changed our lives in a drastic way. Ollie's dad died in Romania while undergoing surgery to remove a cancerous tumor. Socialized medicine in communist Romania was the shortest way to the grave. Ollie eventually managed to bring his mother and sister to the US.

Sometime in 1974, my high school sweetheart Rose and my best friend Pal got married. What a shock! My girlfriend and my best friend were together now, married. My parents sent me a wedding picture of the couple, she in a white dress and he in a dark suit. Neither one of them were smiling. Smiling in a photo was not common during those times. There was not much to smile about, even at a wedding.

I guess my promise to return and marry Rose was like two birds in the bush, while a flesh-and-blood Pal asking to marry her was a bird in hand, indeed. I recovered without any lasting psychological damage or thoughts of revenge. I didn't stay in touch with them after that. Later, I realized that it was a good thing for them to get married. What could be better than for my best friends from my youth to be together!

My escape from Romania traumatized me for many years. After the escape, I had nightmares: nightmares of being caught at the border; nightmares of being back in Romania, as if I had never left; nightmares from which I woke in the middle of the night, drenched in sweat; nightmares that made me get out of bed and run, as if I were trying to escape from some terrifying pursuer. Time cured my horrifying memories, although, I have to say that while I was writing this story, I began reliving it. At times I could feel my heart racing.

I moved to California and found a new job as a design engineer. In the fall of 1975, I enrolled in college at night. I fell in love at first sight with my future wife, Sofia, and we got married in 1976. In 1977, we bought our first house and got a dog and a cat. Having worked in construction in my early days in New York came in handy as a homeowner. In 1978, my wife and I had our beautiful first daughter, Melissa, and then our beautiful second daughter, Michelle, in 1980.

After I became an American citizen, I requested that my parents and sister be permitted to immigrate to the USA. It wasn't an easy undertaking, as the communists would not let people get out of Romania without a fight and many fees, squeezing as many dollars as they could out of you. Because I had left Romania illegally, by law I had lost my Romanian citizenship. Until I became an American citizen, I was a citizen of no country. I wrote to every politician I knew and, lo and behold, my parents and sister received their exit visas, but with one condition: I had to pay, in addition to other fees, to renounce my Romanian citizenship. Wait a second – they had revoked my citizenship already, hadn't they? Well, Romania needed hard currency, dollars, and they used any trick to collect what they thought was owed to them. I paid and sponsored my parents and sister, and they joined me in America in 1981. My family was now complete.

I am a hard worker, and it has paid off. When I was twenty-six years old, I became the manager of the design-engineering department in the company I was working for at that time. I finished university and obtained a degree in industrial management and mechanical engineering. It took me twelve years, going to school at night, but it was worth the perseverance. I climbed the corporate ladder of success, earned decent money, and paid plenty of taxes, like any responsible citizen.

The economic situation back in Romania declined from bad to abysmal by the 1980s. It was to be expected, considering the command-and-control decisions made by bureaucrats in the central government and the lack of incentives to innovate, work hard, and produce more. Communism finally died in Central Europe in 1989, but only after ravaging all those countries.

In Romania, on December 16, 1989, in Timisoara, a group of people came to the aid of the Hungarian-Romanian pastor, Laszlo Tokes, who was being evicted from his apartment for political reasons. The Hungarian religious crowd who were trying to prevent their pastor's eviction were joined by many Romanian folks who began chanting "Liberty" and "Down with Ceausescu." This demonstration happened under the windows of my aunt and uncle's apartment back in Timisoara; they watched it unfold in the street down below.

Where the Revolution started

That small revolt was the spark that started the anti-communist revolution in Romania. All of Romania was a powder keg. In the following days, demonstrations against Ceausescu and the communists increased to the point where the secret police could not control them. The communist party building was burned down, and stores were looted. The military was called into action, and many people were killed. Groups of people demonstrating in front of the cathedral were machine-gunned in cold blood. My aunt remembered people running away from the town center, shouting that many people had been shot near the cathedral.

The Cathedral

The revolt in Timisoara was nearly put down, and many of the demonstrators were arrested. Martial law was imposed on the city. Nighty-eight people were killed, and their bodies were either buried in a mass grave or incinerated to hide the murders committed against the demonstrators. Many more people were wounded, including another uncle of mine. A stray bullet, collateral damage, wounded him in the arm.

Unfortunately for the communists, the whole city rose up, and the military retreated. The communist party recruited workers from Oltenia, a southern region of Romania, armed them with clubs, and transported them by the thousands on trains to squash the revolt in Timisoara. Those workers were told that Hungarian radicals had started the trouble. As it happened, once the club-armed workers arrived in Timisoara and found out that the city was rebelling against the communists, they joined the protesters.

The monument to the fallen heroes

On December 20th, Timisoara declared itself a free city. The news spread throughout Romania like wildfire.

On December 21st, the communist dictator Nicolae Ceausescu ordered 100,000 people in the Palace Square in Bucharest to condemn the revolt in Timisoara, accusing fascists, foreign interventionists, and hooligans as the culprits who started the trouble. Instead of the usual applause and adulation, the crowd's obligatory response to his speech, the people started booing him. Worse yet, the crowd started chanting "Timisoara! Timisoara!" showing solidarity with the besieged free city. The crowd by now knew what had happened and had heard on Voice of America and Radio Free Europe about the atrocities committed by the communists and the military in Timisoara. The people had had enough.

The fear on Ceausescu's face was startling. The people he had controlled so well rose up against him. Down below in the crowd, the revolt had started. Romanian TV captured the whole fiasco, as the speech of the "glorious leader" was transmitted live. It took a few minutes before the transmission was cut off, but Romanians throughout the country witnessed what had happened. Revolts quickly began in other cities.

Nicolae Ceausescu and his wife, Elena, were paralyzed with fear. They were whisked by helicopter out of the capital. The helicopter pilot, claiming possible anti-aircraft fire, landed in a field before reaching their destination. Ceausescu's bodyguard commandeered a car, and they took to the road to escape. They were arrested by the military when they arrived in Targoviste. They were put on trial and on December 25, 1989, Christmas Day, they were found guilty and executed.

A tragic era in Romanian history had come to an end. The fighting continued in the streets for a few more days, in spite of Ceausescu's death. The people had finally won. Over one thousand people died in their efforts to overthrow the monstrous communist regime. Afterward, it turned out that the revolution had started spontaneously, but a faction of communists seized the opportunity to implement a coup d'état against Ceausescu. However, with the fall of the other communist countries, including the Soviet Union, communism in Romania died for good.

Just like all other dictators who are deposed by force, in the end the ones who rule by fear and intimidation end up alone with very few people around them. Remember Saddam Hussein and the rat hole where he ended up all alone? In the end, Nicolae Ceausescu had only his wife Elena with him. She was more hated than he was. Rumor had it that it was she who gave the order to shoot the protestors in Timisoara, while Nicolae Ceausescu was in Iran on a state visit. That's how all these monsters end up before they are put to death.

Thirty-five years after I left, I returned to Romania with my wife to visit my relatives in 2006. It felt surreal to fly from Germany to Timisoara's Traian Vuia International Airport. In customs, I was asked if I held a Romanian passport, even though I was not a Romanian citizen anymore. How times had changed! Now there were many Romanians residing in the West with dual citizenships. Twenty or more years before, I would have been arrested on the spot. Now they smiled at me and said, "*Bine ati venit!*" – Welcome!

My uncle picked us up and, as we drove through Timisoara, it was as if I had never left. The old town was the same. The communists hadn't torn it down, as they did with many old neighborhoods in Bucharest. Timisoara is a beautiful city, built in the Austrian architectural style, and it felt good to be back.

Since communism had collapsed in 1989, Romania was on its way to adapting to a market economy. I was heartened to see Romania as a free country, like any country should be. My friends were all grown up, as old as I was, although they looked older to me, just as I looked older to them. Ned was a professor at the university. Pal owned a hardware store, he was still married to Rose, and they had a daughter. I visited them together with my wife, and we were happy to see each other; we had a lot of stories to share. Everyone else survived the best they could under communism after I left in 1971, but I felt extremely pleased for having made the decision I made when I was eighteen. I feel that I have a better and more fulfilling life in the USA.

My story is a success story, like thousands upon thousands of similar immigrant stories. Do I have any regrets about leaving Romania and becoming an American? None whatsoever. It was the best decision I've ever made in my life.

BOOK 2. COMMUNISM

"Communism is the best political system to spread the misery evenly."

– An anonymous Cuban expatriate

The above quote seems to contradict everything communism stands for: a better life for all. However, people who have experienced communism firsthand – millions of Europeans now free, thousands of Cuban boat people risking their lives to reach Florida, or many more thousands of Vietnamese taking to the high seas to get to freedom – will tell you that communism and misery are one and the same.

Why is communism so appealing? If you are poor, hungry, cold, sick, and unemployed, communism sounds very good. If you see the rich getting richer, flaunting their wealth and living their lives in splendor while you're scraping by, wouldn't you want a fairer political and economic system? Of course you would. We all want a better life, and we would join the communist movement without hesitation, if what it promised would come true.

It is too good to be true. When communism takes over a rich country, that country will become poor, and a poor country will stay poor. Communism and prosperity are incompatible.

Mankind always settles for the optimal cultural, economic, political, and religious system based on our human nature and values. Yes, we are noble, caring, and giving, but we are also greedy, selfish, and envious. We are hard workers, and we are lazy. And all of us do what we do first for personal benefit. That's how God created us.

Unlike communism, philosophers did not invent capitalism. It evolved organically, based on who we are and what each one of us is able to do. Prosperity comes only from work, and the harder we work, the more we'll receive in return. The more we get in return, the harder and smarter we work, and the more prosperous we become. And this fact is made possible only in a capitalist system. Communism will not allow us to prosper from our hard or smart work.

1. WHAT IS COMMUNISM?

"Communism is the most oppressive economic and political system ever devised by man."

As you have read in my story, I risked my life to get out of communism. To the American reader who was born in freedom and democracy, communism may seem mysterious, maybe scary, or perhaps fascinating. What exactly is communism? Communism is a totalitarian and godless political system pretending to represent the people.

There are many books and articles that glorify communism, written here in the free world by "open-minded" individuals who think communism can be rationalized. I have three things to say about people who think communism is acceptable, even desirable:

First, these people don't have real jobs. A real job is to work eight hours a day, and your work produces results for which you are held accountable. Being a TV or radio reporter, or writing editorials or books, are not real jobs. Disseminating subjective opinions, esoteric philosophy, or patronizing judgments about working men and women is not a real job. Being a political science or other liberal arts university professor with tenure is not a real job. No professor is held accountable if students learn or not. When you don't have a real job it is easy to fantasize how the world would be better if we became communists.

Second, none of the people in the free world praising communism have lived under communism as a working person. I don't mean visiting a communist country such as Cuba the way red Hollywood celebrities from producers, directors and actors, have done, and being given the red-carpet treatment, meeting compañero Fidel Castro, and describing what a delight it was to meet him. I wonder any of them would have felt the same way if he had met Adolf Hitler. Hitler and Castro are made from the same cloth. Fidel Castro should be indicted for crimes against humanity for what he has done to the Cuban people.

Fascism-Nazism and Communism are two sides of the same coin.

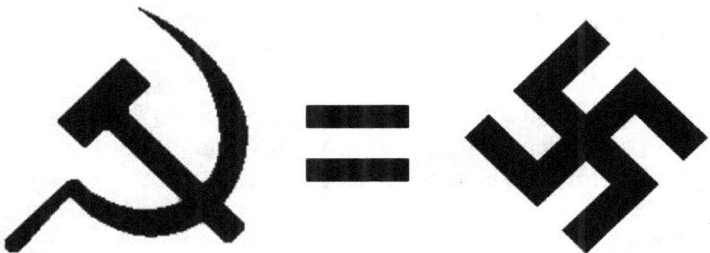

Third, rich people who praise or desire communism are under the false impression that if they live well, so should everyone else under communism. They believe the Marie Antoinette saying, "Let them eat cake," if the poor don't have bread. Some rich people inherited their wealth and have never had a job in their lives. They may feel guilty being rich while others struggle. Why don't they give their money to the poor instead of imposing on the rest of us to be taxed and to fulfill their grandiose communist societies? The newly self-made rich of the entertainment industry, living in the make-believe world of Tinsel Town, believe that communism will make everything better, just like in the happy endings in movies. Sorry for all of you communist-loving rich folks: When communism takes over, your riches will be confiscated and you'll end up in labor camps or executed. I wonder if any of the people mentioned above, while visiting Castro, asked him how many rich people Fidel had executed or thrown in prison? Hypocrites don't ask these kinds of questions. The truth hurts.

No one should glorify communism unless he or she has lived under communism as an ordinary citizen. Every person who has lived under communism will agree with what I've written here, unless they were living as well-placed communist party members.

Communism portrays itself as the government for the working people. In communism there are no rich to exploit the working people, there are jobs for everyone, and the people are taken care of from cradle to grave. You may wonder what's so wrong with a political system that professes equality and a better life for all of us. No classes or castes, no rich or poor, no hunger or suffering, no religion, too. (It sounds like "Imagine" by John Lennon.) In this new environment, we would all work for the common good of society, and we would all prosper together.

Sure, if we were ants or bees it would work, but we are humans, and we live and behave like humans.

In reality, communism is a totalitarian police state, which does not allow any dissent or other political beliefs. It controls all media and propaganda, and only the communist point of view is to be followed. The entire economy is owned by the communist state in the name of the "people," and no private property for profit is allowed. All the people must work only for the government, at preset salaries.

2. CAPITALISM

"It is communism that exploits the people."

To understand communism you need to understand capitalism. Before capitalism, in agrarian societies, land was wealth: If you didn't own land, you were poor. Wealth could be obtained from seafaring commerce or craftsmanship, but with limited success. Land was wealth.

Capitalism was born in the Industrial Revolution. Before the Industrial Revolution, muscle power, that of man or beast, powered just about everything. The mills used waterpower on a limited basis. Wind power was used for sailing, but it wasn't as potent as the steam power that ushered in the machine and the Industrial Revolution. Mass production converting raw materials into goods enriched the bourgeoisie, originally the name for the middle class. The aristocrats and the landowners were the old rich. The bourgeoisie, the factory owners, became the new rich.

Capitalism makes use of five resources: intellect (mind), capital (money), machines, material, and people (men and women). For short, we can call these the five Ms: Mind-Money-Machines-Material-Men. Capitalists put their minds or other people's minds to work, use money to buy machines and materials, and employ workers to produce goods, which are sold for a profit. The capitalists take all the risks, but, if successful, they keep all the profits, and the process is repeated all over for them to gain more prosperity for themselves.

Capitalists start and operate businesses for only one purpose: profits. If capitalists cannot make a profit, they will abandon that business. Capitalists don't start businesses as charities or employment centers. These are the cold facts.

Profits and a more prosperous life are a great incentive to try harder to take the initiative and the financial risks in a capitalist economy. That's why the USA is the strongest economy and not the USSR of the past. Communism deprived people of becoming prosperous, and therefore the people's initiative died, and so did prosperity.

Capitalism also operates in a competitive environment. Competition is not welcome in capitalism, but capitalists have no choice. Competition is started by other entrepreneurs producing the same goods or is imposed by governments to prevent monopolies.

To compete and stay profitably in business, capitalists had to adopt the law of the jungle: the survival of the fittest. However, competition is good for consumers, providing them the best quality and the lowest prices for goods that we enjoy every day.

Competition extends to workers as well. If a business needs eighty workers and there are 300 workers available, the business will hire only the most qualified and hardest working eighty workers. The competition among workers doesn't stop after they are hired. It continues as employees compete among themselves to be promoted and for better wages. The less competitive or less productive employees are fired.

Because there were 300 candidates for the eighty jobs available, capitalists will pay the least possible wages for each worker. It is the law of supply and demand. Too much supply (workers) and not enough demand (jobs) means prices (wages) will go down. If the reverse were to occur, the workers would command higher wages.

Are the business owners providing jobs? No, despite of the fact that business owners and right-wing politicians tout job creation. Jobs are resources that businesses utilize when there is a need, just like material. Business owners are not in business to provide jobs. They are in business to make profits. If a business can prosper without hiring a single employee, it'll do so. It does not seem to be a fair system for providing jobs, but it is the most productive and prosperous way. It seems that we get the best only when businesses or people compete.

Are the business owners exploiting the workers? No, despite what left-wing advocates say. Competition among businesses and workers is what sets wages. If businesses don't have enough workers, they'll raise wages if the market can afford higher-priced goods. If a business pays higher wages to their workers and the competition doesn't, the higher-wage-paying business may go bankrupt, and its workers will be unemployed.

A few years ago, the employees of a local chain grocery store went on strike over medical benefits cutbacks. Management was planning to reduce their contribution to the cost of medical insurance from 100% to 80%, with the rest to be paid by the employees. The union urged the shopping public to boycott these stores during the strike to force management to reconsider. Most of the public sympathized with the store employees and stayed away from those store. But where did the public shop before the strike and during the strike? Probably at the lowest-priced stores. I don't think many shoppers go to the most expensive store to shop because that store pays higher wages and benefits to the employees. Although the public may have sympathized with the employees on strike, they were not willing

142

to shop at the higher-priced stores. We all are part of the market, and we all vote with our wallets, including how much the employees are paid in wages and benefits. The management wanted to stay competitive with other stores by reducing benefits. The employees wanted the same fully paid benefits. Through our shopping habits, we the shoppers decided the matter in reality. Not the management, not the employees.

On what do I base the quote at the beginning of this chapter that says that communism exploits the people? Under communism, all jobs are government jobs – one employer, one owner, one party: the communist party. Salaries are fixed and are based on a pay grade. There is no competition among organizations or employees to offer or obtain better pay. Government, not market forces, sets the salaries. The pay is enough to buy the minimum necessities, if you can find them in the stores. The government distributes the goods in the stores as well. Communism puts people to work, but pays all workers equally regardless of how hard they work, and sells them the goods to survive.

In a free-market economy, the market sets the prices for goods and, consequently, for employment rates and wages. Every time one of us buys something, we affect the market, whether we shop at discount stores or high-fashion boutiques. We all are part of the market.

3. THE PROLETARIAT AND THE COMMUNIST REVOLUTION

The good news: No more rich to exploit the working people.

The bad news: The communists exploit all the people now.

Capitalism seems to be a cruel and unjust economic system. The rich capitalists live lives of privilege and carefree abundance. The workers, the proletariat, on the other hand, are poor, hungry, and suffering. It is not fair.

Well, two bearded 19th-century philosophers, Karl Marx and Friedrich Engels, pronounced that the rich, who control the capital and the businesses, exploit the workers, and that the amassing of capital by a few is unfair. There is a better system: Let's do away with the rich, but not with the businesses and the jobs. Who is to say that only the rich can create jobs? Why not have a government of the people take over the entire economy and become a fair and honest employer? And although the gains will be modest, they will be shared equally with everyone, and no one will be allowed to become rich and exploit his fellow man. In theory, that sounds marvelous!

In 1917, the Bolsheviks, under Vladimir Ilyich Lenin, took power in Russia through revolution, and then they had the chance to implement the proletariat state. The Soviet Union

144

became the first communist state. Similar revolutions took place in China and other countries in Asia later on. After the end of World War II, the Soviet Union occupied and forced the Central European nations into communism through fraudulent elections. Stalin allegedly said, "It's not the people who vote that count. It's the people who count the votes." For someone who was never elected, he knew a thing or two about counting the votes in communists' favor.

From that point on, communism was not a philosophical theory anymore, but a practical political system in Europe and elsewhere. The communist system abolished private wealth, and the state became the owner of everything.

4. COMMUNISM'S CONSOLIDATION OF POWER

"The communists don't own anything; they own everything."

Taking over power in a country by revolution or fraudulent election is only the first step. Communism as a political system must have absolute power and control of the government, military, police, media and information, education, and economy. The totalitarian communist entity is one party, one rule, and total control, even of the minds of the people. Once in power, the communists will not let go of it.

The security of the communist state is crucial. The communist party takes control of the police and military. All the officers in the police and military must become communist party members, or they're fired. The communist party is entrenched in the military by assigning political commissars to supervise the officers. The military is first and foremost loyal to the communist party, not the nation. Together with the police, the communist government will be well guarded against the people it supposedly represents.

All other political parties are abolished, their leaders are jailed and eventually executed, and no dissent against the communist party is allowed. There is no political freedom. After all, the communist party represents the people, and the party knows best what's good for the people.

Information and propaganda institutions become the monopoly of the communist party. All other sources of news are shut down and, if anyone disseminates any news or propaganda that is not sanctioned by the party, that person or persons are arrested, imprisoned, or executed.

The last and most difficult aspect of controlling a population is the minds of the people. The communists cannot confiscate a mind. But they can influence and brainwash the people. First on their agenda is to minimize or outright eliminate the influence of the church. Religion is a mighty competitor. It tells us all that God is supreme. No! Communism is supreme. There must be no God, no hope for a better life, even after death.

However, the religions know a lot about mind control. And this fact was not lost on the communists. Who is more religious, a person who goes to church at least once a week and reads the Bible, or the person who attends church once a year? To indoctrinate people, the party adopted many of religion's practices: First, enlist as many people as possible in the communist party, and afterward purge the undesirables or the opportunists. The god for communist party members is communism. The members have to learn about the communist doctrine and behave accordingly. The party members attend mandatory weekly meetings to continuously be indoctrinated and reminded about communist principles. And at every meeting they sing the "Internationale," the communist hymn. Each party member keeps an eye on everyone else to ensure that no one verbalizes anti-communist feelings. The practice of communism is no different than the practice of religion, except that it is in the name of a fictitious god called communism.

How about the non-communist members? They, too, are subject to political meetings, though not as frequently, conducted through schools and employment. The communist party members are responsible to spread the "communist gospel" every time they have a chance. And if anyone steps out of line, expressing dissent or different political views, or denigrating the leadership, they are to be reported to the secret police. The secret police will correct the *incorrect* thinking.

The ultimate problem with communism is that it must have total control of everything. In this type of closed political system, the biggest psychopaths rise to power. Psychopathic leaders like Stalin, Mao, Ceausescu, Pol Pot, Castro, and many other communist leaders were, are, and will be so skilled at controlling their inner circle of top cadre communists that no one dares overturn them. So they stayed or stay in power like parasites on their prey.

Stalin and his secret police chief Beria routinely worked late at night to select the names of intellectuals who were deemed dangerous. The next day those people were arrested, and, after full confessions under torture, they were shot. Imagine the president of the United States working with the head of the Secret Service to identify his opponents and execute them. In communism this is easy to do. Who is going to protest? If you do, you'll be shot next.

5. NATIONALIZATION

"The theory of the communists may be summed up in the single sentence: 'Abolition of private property' and '...the exploitation of one individual by another is put to an end...'"

– Karl Marx, *the Communist Manifesto*

Personal wealth is abolished, and it becomes the property of the government. The entire economy is nationalized, and the government, in the name of the people, is the new and sole owner. Manufacturing organizations with thousands of employees or one-employee shops are confiscated from their owners. All real estate, commerce, transportation, warehousing, distribution, and retail shops are nationalized. All mineral resources, land, and agriculture become the property of the government. All banking and financial institutions are expropriated by the government. In short, the communist government becomes the sole owner of the entire economy of a country. No single individual or groups of individuals have financial power over the communist government from that point on.

The land taken from the rich landowners becomes the property of the government, and the peasants work for the government, not for rich landlords. The peasants maintain their same fate, not much different than it was before the communists took over. Besides rich landowners, there are landowning peasants. Confiscating thousands of acres from one owner is easy. Confiscating a few acres from each of the thousands of peasants is not. Peasants have fought for centuries to get a plot of their own. Land ownership is sacred to them.

The collectives are formed to appease the peasants that their land is not confiscated, but aggregated in a more efficient enterprise; together they would work the land and prosper from their work together. A large farm is more efficient than hundreds of individual farms. True, except, would the peasants work harder on their own plot or the collective's plot?

When landowning peasants in the Ukraine refused to collectivize in the Soviet Union in the 1930s, Stalin starved millions of them until they complied with the collectivization. Owning food was a crime during that time, and only the government could own it and distribute it.

You may think, I don't own a business, I don't own a bank, and I don't own land. I am an employee, working for an institution, which might be the government. What do I care about the nationalization of other people's assets?

Unless they take your house. Would they do that? All properties could be nationalized. Most likely it depends on how big your real estate is: If you own a duplex, you can stay in one unit but lose the other one. You cannot exploit a renter, but the government can. If you have a large house with many bedrooms and only two of you live in it, some of the bedrooms will be given to other needy people. The kitchen will be for common use.

But look on the bright side: You are lucky that they left you with the master bedroom and bathroom. At least you won't have to share the bathroom in the hallway.

So why should you care about nationalization? If you don't own assets today, under communism you'll never be able to acquire any revenue-producing assets. Imagine when everything is the property of the government. Have you tried to fight city hall? Is the government efficient? It takes at least two bureaucrats to do the job of a privately employed worker. The wealth of a society depends on how productive we the workers are. If we all slack off, the entire nation slides into poverty.

You may still think it is not fair for private individuals to own assets, to be rich while other people are poor. However, only a private owner will care enough and make sure that his or her business is prosperous. In a pervasive way, if individuals own private property and they are prosperous, so will everyone else be, too.

The incentive of being able to gain riches and keep them without overtaxation gives many people, men and women, the initiative to try harder, starting with one's choice of profession and education, then working harder in a job or starting a business. Take the incentive away, and the initiative dies. When the initiative dies, our prosperity dies.

The media ridiculed the trickle-down economy. When the government owns everything and there are no more wealthy people, there will be nothing to trickle down. Communism proved that in any country they controlled or control.

6. KILLING THE OPPOSITION

"If you are not with communism, you are against communism, and you will be eliminated."

Hitler was a mass murderer. He killed 11 million civilians in his effort to cleanse his perfect society of "undesirables." However, the number of people he killed pales in comparison with how many people the communists have killed to enforce and protect their regimes. Joseph Stalin killed more than 30 million of his own people; Mao Zedong killed more than 45 million; Pol Pot killed 2 million in the killing fields of Cambodia, more than one-fifth of the country's population. Imagine a dictator in the US killing 60 million Americans because they are of another mind.

Communist Romania killed 300,000 of its most productive and hardworking citizens in labor camps. And the same happened in Hungary, Poland, Bulgaria, Czechoslovakia, Albania, and East Germany. Let's not get dramatic here: Who cares about millions of dead Russians, Chinese, Cambodians, Romanians, and or other Central Europeans who, for being industrious or resisting communism, were tortured, shot, or starved to death? It was done in the name of the greater good of the people, the communists claim.

You may think all these killings happened in the past; communism is not that way anymore. The killings continue today in North Korea, China, Viet Nam and Cuba. No, not on the Mao's scale, because the population has been cowered in accepting the communist rule and the lives of slaves. Communism is an absolutist system, no opposition is allowed. You either comply or you die.

These killings mentioned above happen shortly after the communists come into power. These people are the anti-communists and all other opposition parties, including the socialists (yes, socialists; they are leftist competitors) and the opposing media. The rich are killed during nationalization if they fight back. Other rich people die of shock or heart attacks, like my grandfather did after seeing his life's work confiscated. But the vast majority of them are deported to labor camps where they die of starvation, illnesses, cold, and exhaustion. If religious leaders stand up for the believers, they are eliminated swiftly. If landowning peasants don't give up their land and refuse to join in, many are killed through starvation during collectivization.

When it comes to political beliefs, people fall into three categories:

The Naïve, the vast majority

The Idealists, a large number

The Shrewd, a minority

During any political movement, the idealists fire up the naïve, who rise and follow the idealists for the benefit of the shrewd.

155

That's what happens in a revolution. All of us fall into one of these categories, although at one time or another we may take any of the other characteristics. I, for one, am a naïve. I believe what I'm told. That doesn't mean I haven't been an idealist, or even a shrewd, at one time or another. Life forces you to change when there is a need.

Communists understand how people behave. Among the communists there are plenty of idealists, envisioning a better world. The idealists change the naïves' minds to join them in the fight against injustice. Many of the naïve die in the struggle, and, once victory is achieved, the shrewd shed their sheepskins and take control of the leadership.

After the communists have eliminated the opposition and after the nationalization, while in full control of a country, the second wave of killings and imprisonments begins. The second wave of killings or labor re-education incarcerations are taken against the minorities, like the Jews, and the intellectuals: yes, all of academia, especially liberal arts and humanities professors, writers, teachers, and professionals of theoretical knowledge.

This sounds preposterous. It is mostly the intellectuals who promoted, supported, demonstrated, and rallied for the communists' success. Yes, but idealists and intellectuals think. A thinking mind is a dangerous mind for communists. Karl Marx was an idealist, and he would have been executed if he had been alive under communism, just like Leon Trotsky, another idealist, who was murdered in Mexico at the orders of Stalin, the shrewd. Che Guevara was an idealist; Fidel Castro is the shrewd.

But why kill the idealists?

Intellectuals want all humanity to live in a better world by imagining utopian (artificial) political and behavioral systems.

Communism is a utopian system. There is a big difference between cloud dreaming and putting communism into practice at ground level. When communism becomes reality, it becomes pure hell.

Intellectuals want a better world. Communism is not a "better" world, and soon they realize the communists in power have duped them. The intellectuals demonstrated in the streets for a better world, and they'll do or try to do so again. In a capitalist system, they are allowed to demonstrate and scream their demands in our faces. They are not allowed to do the same under communism. If any intellectual thinks he or she had it rough under capitalism, communism will be a nightmare. And the salaries will be smaller, too.

The sinister truth is that the teachers will receive special treatment. They will be "re-educated" to believe and obey the communist doctrine. If they resist, they will be eliminated, or incarcerated. At the minimum they will not be allowed to teach again. The teachers who comply become the instrument of indoctrination and brainwashing of the young minds. New truths, new history, and a new way of life will be thought. God disappears and communism becomes the new "god." All religious holidays are banned and even simple wishes such as Merry Christmas are prohibited; in this respect I believe we in the USA are almost there.

Artists, musicians, and especially writers will face a new reality. Where before they were able to express themselves freely, under communism they can express only what the party allows them. Why especially writers? Writing is at the heart of propaganda, and just as the communists used written propaganda to grab power, they will not allow the same approach against them. In communist Romania, the writers, besides being told what to write and being censored, were obligated to include Ceausescu's words of wisdom in their

157

books, whether the words were related to the book's subject or not.

Would any writer in the US be interested in including their most disliked American president's words of wisdom in his or her book and praising that president?

After the late-1960s, communists did not have to resort to mass killings anymore in Central Europe. They were well entrenched as the sole government, and the population was indoctrinated or scared into complying with what the communist government wished. The situation was the same in communist Romania under Nicolae Ceausescu. He did not have to massacre anyone. Gheorghe Gheorgiu Dej, his predecessor, did all the necessary killing. However, Ceausescu was not a saint. He and his secret police kept the prisons filled with political dissidents. For the more bothersome troublemakers, he relied on a more subtle way of killing them, using radioactivity. A small radioactive pellet placed under the dissident's bed in prison would ensure some form of cancer would develop in the person's body. After a short period of time, as if by natural causes, the prisoner died of cancer, and not at the hands of the secret police.

Communism is an absolutist system, and people are not regarded as individuals with rights but as entities to be used and discarded as needed for the glory of communism.

7. Is Communism That Bad?

"The best thing about communism:

There is no welfare. Everyone must work, whether they like it or not."

"The worst thing about communism:

Everyone works for the government, and nothing gets done."

Communism is from the people and for the working people. In communism, there are no rich to exploit us, there are jobs for everyone, and we are taken care of from cradle to grave. (Actually, in communist Romania you had to pay for your own burial. Once dead, the state had no more use for you.)

A similar system existed once in the USA. It was called slavery. The plantation owner gave jobs to all his slaves, fed and clothed them, and cared for them, too, as much as one cares for his property. If a slave stepped out of line, proper punishment was administered swiftly and efficiently, from beatings to execution. The slaves had no choice but to do as the master decreed and work for the master until death. No other alternatives were available. If a slave tried to escape, he would be caught and his head would end up on a pike as an example to the others.

Communism is supposed to make life for the common man and woman better. Even I recognize that when I was growing up, I did not go hungry, I had medical attention, and my schools were free, and everyone had jobs. True, but let's look at each one of these as they are applied in real life:

Hunger. I had food to eat. No, not 99 different cereals to choose from for breakfast, but food, mostly milk and bread. My parents made sure that I was well fed. A kid will always go to sleep hungry if the parent(s) do not care about him or her. In the US, the demagogues tell us that millions of kids go to bed hungry in America, with the subliminal message that the rich are starving our kids or we have an unfair system. America is a rich country, and, with the amount of social welfare available, no kid should be going to bed hungry. What those kids are lacking is not availability of food but proper parenting. Kids don't go hungry in this country because the rich are getting richer at the kids' expense, but because their parents are unfit to be parents.

Basic food staples were available in communist Romania, some in more abundance than others, for which people had to wait in long lines, come rain or come shine. Vegetables and fruits were available only in season. The variety of food was limited, and most of the daily diet was about the same. I recall my daily diet being bread and milk in the morning; a sandwich with lard, or butter and marmalade, for lunch; and bread with fried potatoes or cabbage, or soups, for dinner. On Sundays, my family had a chicken or other meat in soups or stews. And my mom baked a cake for sweets. Try this diet for a month. One benefit is that you might lose weight.

You may think that there are lots of nations out there so poor that what we had to eat would be a banquet for them. Romania before World War II was not a poor country. None of the Central European countries that were made communist by the Soviet

161

Union were poor. After the war and with communist governments in charge, it was all but assured that they would become poor. And if a poor nation thinks that communism will bring prosperity, think again, because that nation will stay poor.

Health care. Socialized medicine is free, and doctors, hospitals, and drugs are available for all. At least that's the theory, and it would be nice if it were a reality. As a kid I received my vaccines and general checkups. And that was good. But if it was something more advanced, I'm not sure I would have fared well. For years when I was a kid I had sinus and ear infections, which were not cured until I outgrew them. Or the time when I received a tetanus injection, and I had to be taken to the hospital later that night, unable to breathe and covered in water blisters, because of poor drug quality.

Dentists were not any better. It seems that pulling teeth out was the preferred method of fixing diseased teeth – why operate when you can amputate? When I was a kid, I broke one of my front teeth chopping wood. The dentist removed the nerve, filled the hole, and left me with a half-broken tooth without capping it. That tooth eventually wore down to my gum line. Later on, I broke the other front tooth during a wrestling match. My parents had to pay – it wasn't free – to have the dentist mount a bridge and give me a half-decent dental appearance. One of my new teeth was silver metal. That was very becoming in communism.

In communist Romania, all doctors were government employees. They were paid a salary, set by the government, and had no way of earning more, even if they worked harder. What's the incentive to see forty patients a day versus twenty a day when the pay is the same? So the waiting rooms were always overcrowded, with coughing and suffering individuals. If you were older, if you needed surgery, or if you had to stay in the hospital for extended periods of time, your chances of coming out alive were low.

Back in Romania, one of my aunts had a heart attack and was taken to the hospital. She was declared well and was to be discharged the following day. My uncle went to the hospital to take her home, but her bed was empty, and no one knew her whereabouts. They finally found her – in the morgue. She had died during the night and the next of kin, my uncle or her daughters, never knew. Nurses and doctors don't much care what happens once their shifts are over. So people die. No repercussions, no problems. Those are the kind of results you can expect from government-run medical establishments.

The miserable state of socialized medicine in communism is not because of bad doctors or bad training, but because of the inherent lack of accountability and lack of modern medications and modern equipment. It was the entire system at fault. There is only so much money to care for an inexhaustible supply of the sick. In communism, there is even less money than in capitalism.

To get proper care from socialized medicine and live, a solution is always available. It is called a *bribe*. You bribe the doctor and nurses, and you'll be taken care of, instead of dying. But this is not free medicine anymore, is it? What happens to the people who don't have money? They die. Life expectancy in communist Romania was sixty-six years of age – so much for socialized medicine.

Free schools. My parents didn't pay a dime for me to go to school. However, I had to take a competitive exam to go to high school. There were limited places for high school, and many kids never attended high school, free as it was. It was even more competitive to go to university. If you cannot attend high school and later college, what difference does it make if the school is free? You cannot attend, period. And there were no private schools.

Not everyone needs to become a philosopher or study liberal arts with no chance of getting a job in their field. True, why spend money on education that will not have a payback? But that should be an individual's choice, not the government's. Besides, an educated population makes a better society, but not in communism. An educated society will start questioning the leadership of the country when things are going bad. That is not allowed. Communists need doers, not thinkers and independent minds. Were there no educated people in communist countries? Sure there were, but only as planned and to keep the economy sputtering along.

Jobs. Since a communist government eliminates all private ownership of assets and becomes the only employer in that country, it has an obligation to provide for its citizens. Hungry people tend to rebel, so there must be jobs, and jobs for everyone. Unemployment has been eliminated. Unless you are totally disabled, you must work to eat. Everyone must work. No exceptions.

In a capitalist economy, unemployment soars during economic declines, creating financial hardships for many people. Full employment appears to be a dream come true in communism. However, this is the biggest misconception about jobs and communism.

Under capitalism, if you were to lose your job, you would be entitled to unemployment compensation until you found another job. Under communism, there is no unemployment or unemployment compensation. A job will be given to you and you must work for the same pay as the unemployment compensation. In other words, you don't stay home and receive money while searching for an equal or better job, you go and work at a job if you want to get paid, and this job pays the same as the unemployment pay you would get in capitalism. But at least you'll get a job.

164

Great! Go to the employment placement center and they'll give you a job. No multiple job openings to choose from, and if there are several openings, the pay is the same. What are the chances that you'll like the job they'll pull out of the hat? Say you work as a clerk in an office: Nice, warm, and cozy, but what if you lose your job for no particular reason? The government will provide you with another job, clerical, of course. But it is at the other end of town, in an unheated warehouse. If you don't take it, you won't eat. OK, you'll take it, while in the meantime you search for something better. But non-working people, not working people like you, are given first priority for job openings. There are plum jobs, but those are available only for people related or connected to the right communist party members. So you either stay unhappily where you were assigned or bribe people at the employment center to give you a more desirable job. Nepotism, corruption, and bribes work well in communism.

Limitations and scarcities are a byproduct of the communist system. There is no private ownership of commerce or finances in communism. Therefore everything is owned by the state. Imagine the entire population of the US working for Uncle Sam: Do you think the government is efficient, even the US government? Not now, or ever.

8. How a Rich Country Becomes Poor under Communism

"Communism will make a rich country poor, and a poor country will stay poor."

In capitalism a few people are extremely rich, many are middle class, and the rest are poor. Therefore, if you take the money from the rich and give it to the poor, the poor will be better off financially. As for the rich, they get what they deserve, nothing. And if they're lucky the communists won't hang them with the ropes the capitalists sold them in the first place; I'm paraphrasing Lenin here.

The following is a simplified, hypothetical example of what happens when communism takes over and the rich lose their wealth in the US. The new owner of all assets is the communist state. Take one of those super rich guys; his name is John Billionaire III. He is worth a cool billion dollars in assets, which can be summed up as follows:

Personal residences in four states: valued at $40 million

Luxury apartment building in downtown Manhattan: valued at $250 million

Municipal bonds: valued at $400 million

Stocks: valued at $300 million

Cash, gold, and jewelry: valued at $60 million

Gross earned income: $41 million per year, for which he pays 20% in taxes, or $8.2 million

Life is good for John Billionaire III. But the greed and the ill-gotten wealth of the likes of him cause a revolution in the US, and the Communist Party of America takes over the government of the former USA. The name for this new glorious country is the United Soviets of America, or the USA. (*Soviet* is the Russian word for council.)

The first thing the party does is nationalize all industry, commerce, banking, transportation, agriculture, in short, all the economy of the US. All assets in the US belong to the communist government, which in turn is for the benefit of the entire population. Sounds good, and good riddance to all those superrich. Power to the people!

John Billionaire III is quick on his feet and grabs all his cash, jewelry, and gold and flees to China, a new safe haven for the ex-superrich. He takes with him $60 million. However, the rest of his assets are frozen in the United Soviets of America. So $940 million can be redistributed from one rich guy to the poor many. Long lives communism!

Really? Here is what will happen. His four residences, worth $40 million, are not worth as much. There are no more rich people to buy them, and therefore their value drops to the replacement cost. But that's irrelevant because those mansions

167

become the residences of higher-up communists. Nothing is available for redistribution to the poor.

Let's take the luxury apartment building before nationalization. The building has 100 luxury apartments, and the yearly revenue is $25 million. Stockbrokers, making seven-figure salaries, occupied these apartments, affording the average of $20,000+ rent per month. The valuation of this building was $250 million. (It's simple arithmetic: take the yearly income and multiply by 10.)

After nationalization, the stock market is eliminated. There are no private investors anymore. The 100 stockbrokers who occupied the apartments are unemployed, and they cannot afford a fraction of the previous rent, so they vacate. They move in with their parents. The apartment building generates zero revenue now. Eventually, other people will move in, but they can pay more like $2,000 per month in rent instead of $20,000. The luxury apartment building's value drops to $25 million, if someone could buy it, but there are no private investors. Again, there is no money left over to give away.

The municipal bonds valued at $400 million are worthless. The new communist government annuls them, along with all other instruments of debt issued by former federal, state, and municipal governments.

The stock valued at $300 million is worthless as well. All businesses were nationalized. The stockholders have been nationalized in the process, and they were wiped out. The buildings and machinery of the businesses may have replacement value. But there are many businesses, such as investment banking or insurance companies, among others, that will be worthless in the case of nationalization. There are no investment bankers in communism.

Let's do the math. John Billionaire III was worth a cool billion. He took (the preferred communist lingo is "he stole") $60 million of his own money and fled to China. The only things of value left behind are the houses, apartment building, and some industry. So $940 million has been reduced to not much, other than real estate, industrial buildings, and machinery, which could not be sold to anyone. All this because the old economic system was replaced with a communist-government-own-it-all new system. Where are all those riches promised for redistribution to the people? They vanished.

You may think, something does not add up here. The government nationalized all the businesses; therefore, the government owns the $300 million in stocks now. Well, $300 million was the value of the stocks. The businesses (brick and mortar) have a tangible value, but not nearly their former value. It's a situation similar to that of the luxury apartment building and the private residences.

How about the municipal government bonds? The local governments no longer owe $400 million. The excused liability amounts to $400 million in credit for those governments. That's true: The governments do not have to pay back the principal plus interest. But what did they do with the $400 million they originally borrowed? Did they use that money to invest wisely, or did they borrow to pay yesterday's liabilities? If I have $40,000 in credit card charges that I spent on wine, women, and song in Las Vegas, after my debt is forgiven I am still asset-less. The only thing I've gained is no more monthly credit card charges, which are a fraction of the original money I owed.

Therefore, when we look at all the wealth in the hands of the rich, is that wealth tangible, cold cash? Only a part of that is tangible. Is this fake wealth? No, that's how capitalism assesses the value of the assets, a valuation based on supply and demand. At a single point in time, if John Billionaire III wanted to "cash out," he would have been able to sell his assets, apartment building, stocks, and bonds and receive close to the book value for his assets. But if every billionaire would do the same thing at the same time, they would get almost nothing for their assets. The supply of assets for sale would far surpass the demand and available cash.

Therefore, what's left after communism takes over is the infrastructure that can house and employ the population. But that's what the people had before communism's takeover, and nothing else.

9. THE STANDARD OF LIVING GOES DOWN

*"Under communism there is no profit. But profit is the gauge
for efficiency and productivity."*

On the bright side, people have jobs. Yes, they do, and
everyone, except for John Billionaire III, will have jobs. The
state has to provide jobs since there is no unemployment
compensation or welfare or food stamps. You're a single mother
with seven kids? No problem. The state provides childcare, and
the mother goes to work. The childcare will be one step above
an orphanage, but it is free.

You're sixty years old and unemployed? No problem, a job
will be provided and you must work until the retirement age of
sixty-five or sixty-six. The pay may be the same as
unemployment or welfare compensation, but you must work;
you cannot stay home and receive free money. Everyone must
work, whether they like it or not.

The 100 brokers' parents lost all their retirement savings, since most of it was invested in stocks and bonds, which are now worthless. They cannot support their former stockbroker children, who will have to move out. All retirees will have to live on their Social Security. The people who saved all their lives lost it all, and they will live on the same pension as the people who saved nothing.

The 100 stockbrokers will be given jobs. No, not the seven-figure salaries they used to get. As a matter of fact, all the well-paid jobs will be reduced. What kind of work did the former brokers do? Clerical is the closest skill that comes to mind. But there are no clerical position openings in Manhattan. No problem: By government decree, the companies that employ clerks will make room for these newcomers. And if a company never had clerical jobs before, it'll have to create some new ones. Similar things happen to other professions, and jobs are created for the sake of creating jobs.

You don't have to be a financial genius to realize that, if one employee performed a job before and now it takes two, something has to give. Either each employee takes a 50% pay cut, or the prices of the products will rise, causing inflation. None of that will happen under communism. The brokers will get paid the same as the existing clerks, and retail prices for essential necessities such as food and everyday goods will be frozen at the pre-communist level. The other non-essential products' prices will skyrocket if they remain unsold in the stores. Many people have some cash, but soon the cash will be spent on hard-to-find products at higher prices.

Who will be financing this new economic system? The communist government owns the banks now, and they can print money as easily as the capitalist government before them did, but without the repercussion of inflation because the government controls the salaries and prices of goods. The

173

government also controls the quantity and the variety of products available for consumers. Too much money in people's hands, and the government makes the products unavailable or raises the prices. The communist money becomes worthless paper money.

The United Soviets of America dollar will become worthless worldwide, but that is not an immediate concern since imported goods are not necessities. Although this may work for a short while, it will not work for long. Productivity and market principles cannot be ignored, and they will come back and bite big. Everyone works for little pay with which they can buy necessities. Shortages and bad quality will become the norm.

Who owns the businesses, a factory, for example? The government. Who is the government? An entity (the proverbial city hall), no one in particular. Who manages a business? A manager, at first the same one working under a private owner, although his salary is reduced since he was "overpaid" in the first place, and along with him all other "overpaid" employees will see their pay cut. If the manager did not do a good job in the past, the owner of the business would fire him. If the manager does not do a good job now, will he be fired? He could be, if he is in bad standing with the overseeing party members, or he does not become a party member. If he is in good standing, he will not be fired. Therefore, what's the incentive for the manager to do the best job, if his salary was cut and he has no accountability, and his laziness is not punished? He and all the other workers slack off. It starts at the top, the manager is just an employee, and it flows down to our fictitious two clerks. Not only was their workload cut in half, but lack of accountability soon causes them to slow down even more. Because of that, another clerk is needed and hired. One employee once did the job; now it takes three. And so it is with every other job.

In a free society, when it comes to accumulating wealth, people fall into three categories: the people who do, the people who don't, and the people who want or try to do. The people who do are the entrepreneurs and the business owners. The people who don't are the employees. And the people who want or try to do are the employees who aspire to become the doers. This categorization is not to place a stigma on one's personality; it reflects one's level of comfort (not necessarily hard work) when applied to work.

The doers don't have to be rich. A plumber with a van and the entrepreneurial spirit makes him a businessman. A pastry chef with an oven at home and the entrepreneurial spirit makes her a businesswoman. And the don'ts need not be poor. There are well-to-do employees, too. I, for one, tried very hard to start several enterprises, but I wasn't successful. I guess that makes me a want or try to do. I learned one thing: It takes extreme effort and hard work to be a doer.

The problem with communism is that it transforms everyone into don'ts, or employees. A prosperous society needs and allows its people to become doers. Without this freedom there would be no Microsoft or Bill Gates, Apple or Steve Jobs, and Amazon or Jeff Bezos, just to mention a very few of the many who have transformed our economy in modern times. Without allowing people to excel and become personally wealthy, the economy and prosperity will stagnate and decline.

Lack of productivity results in shortages and bad quality. People have paper money but not much to buy with it, except the necessary staples of crappy quality. Shortages are sometimes affected by pure negligence on the part of the workers. Bad quality creates shortages as well. It takes about the same amount of time to produce a bad product as it takes for a good one. So instead of having 100 products shipped to market, only fifty may be shipped because of quality defects. But the work was performed and was paid for 100 units.

Without a true owner who cares for that business, nobody is in charge. Most employees leave at the end of the workday and do not care about their place of employment. To some degree, this is true in a capitalist system as well. However, the owners and their deputies care 24/7, and they will keep on top of all aspects of their businesses. That makes a big difference when it comes to efficient production and the quality of goods as reflected by profits.

A true story: My father-in-law had a coffee-roasting and - packing business in Nicaragua. He employed half a dozen people. Not a big business, but he and six employees earned a living. The Sandinistas took over the government in Nicaragua, ousting Somoza in the late 1970s. Although the Sandinistas were not originally communists, by the time they won, they were communists supported by Cuba. Shrewd Daniel Ortega eliminated the idealist Sandinistas.

A couple of communist zealots employed at the coffee-packing business, emboldened by the Sandinista revolution, took it upon themselves to "nationalize" the small coffee business. In other words, they confiscated my father-in-law's business. He had no recourse, so he immigrated to Costa Rica, losing the business he and his wife had built from nothing over the period of a lifetime.

But that's not the end of the tragedy. A week later, the small factory burned down. All the workers were the owners now, and they didn't have to take orders from a single owner who kept close watch on his business. They were owners in name, but in their minds they were employees. A worker/owner left a roasting oven on, and the building caught on fire. The equipment, inventory, and records were incinerated. Six people

176

became unemployed because of the employee mentality of one of the so-called owners. The factory was never rebuilt. There was no true owner anymore.

Karl Marx said, "From each according to his abilities, to each according to his needs." Translation: Engels can produce twice as much, because he has the ability to work harder. Marx cannot produce as much, but he has a great appetite and he needs to eat double portions. This is one of the major flaws of communism. If you can work hard, you should work hard, but if another is lazy, he should be given a job and not starve. How long do you think it will take for the hardworking to wise up and slow down? Imagine an entire nation doing that.

When I went back to Romania in 2006, I noticed what people were saying. They were happy to see communism gone, but were not happy to have to work hard. They also didn't see the relationship between productivity and wages. Unproductive jobs were disappearing, and that caused hardships and unemployment. The state was no longer able to provide pretend jobs for which people received pretend salaries.

In just two generations, communism had destroyed the work ethic of the Romanian people. It did the same thing in all communist countries, including East Germany, while West Germany prospered. During World War II, the allies bombed Germany to heaps of rubble. But the allies did not destroy the work ethic of the German people. West Germany rose up through hard work and became the fourth largest economy in the world. The Soviet Union did not bomb the Central European countries, but its communist system destroyed the work ethic of the population.

The methodical destruction of the work culture sewn into the communist system is what caused the implosion of the European communist states. How long will it take for the

Central European countries to recover and rebuild? At least one generation, if not more. Young people will have to grow up in a free economy to understand what it takes to prosper, and that is hard work and continuing freedom.

How about China? It is communist, and it is the second largest economy in the world, and soon, some say, it may be the largest, surpassing the USA. Chinese communists, as of the late 20th century, became pragmatists, and, as they put it, changed China to a socialist market economy. Maybe Mao's Cultural Revolution in the 1960s and '70s convinced the younger communists that prosperity and communism couldn't coexist. I have to use again one of those gems of utopian wisdom of Karl Marx's from *The Communist Manifesto*: "Communism deprives no man of the ability to appropriate the fruits of his labor. The only thing it deprives him of is the ability to enslave others by means of such appropriations." The Chinese communists took to heart the first sentence and struck off the second one. Or, as it is attributed to Deng Xiaoping, "To get rich is glorious."

The Chinese communists realized that where there are no profits, there is no prosperity. As a consequence, there are Chinese billionaires now in communist China. Mao would turn over in his grave if he knew what had happened to his Cultural Revolution.

And so the Chinese socialist market economy seems to finally marry communism and prosperity successfully. As long as the Chinese people are earning a living because of low labor costs, the communists are safely in power, and the people will not mind the lack of freedom and liberty. What will happen when the Chinese economy will falter, or they have to compete on an equal footing with the rest of the world, and prosperity stagnates or even declines? Will the communist government be able to stay in power? Time will tell.

10. WHY COMMUNISM IS DOOMED TO FAIL

"If it is not specifically allowed, it is illegal."

The problem with communism is that it always assumes power in a country by force or electoral fraud. (Chile, under Allende, was the exception.) Humans are not perfect; we make mistakes, and politicians are no different. It is one thing for you and me to make a mistake in our respective lives and suffer the consequences, and another for the government to make a mistake and an entire nation suffers the consequences. When politicians make mistakes, they are voted out of power. The problem with communism is that, when communists make mistakes, the people cannot vote the sons of bitches out of power.

A clique of the shrewdest party members establishes itself in power like a new aristocracy. They live the good life and are far removed from the daily lives of the ordinary people they claim to serve. They make decisions with little concern for the outcomes and how the population will be affected. The old aristocratic/capitalist hierarchy is replaced with the new communist hierarchy. Communism works for the communists only when they have absolute and total power. In other words, it is their way and *no highway*; you stay where you are and do as you're told, as in slavery.

At the very top, the elite party members are in charge of the government and everything it possesses, in other words, everything. They now live a life of splendor and abundance. Below them is the inner circle of higher-up party members, politicians masquerading as the representatives of the people. In reality, they are the rubber-stamp congress. Below them are the intelligentsia, the educated elites, management, military, police, and all other party members. And last in line is the vast majority of the equally poor, the general population, which has no say and no power to do anything about their lives or their government.

Based on the many states an individual can live in, a lack of individual freedom would rank as follows:

1. Prisoner (no political, civil, or economic freedom or freedom of movement)
2. Slave (no political or civil freedom; minor economic freedom and freedom of movement)
3. Communism (no political freedom; minor civil and economic freedom, and limited freedom of movement only within national borders)
4. Theocracies (no political or civil freedom; economic freedom and freedom of movement, but limited for international travel)
5. Nazism (no political freedom; some civil freedom; economic freedom and freedom of movement, but only for the approved race or nationality)
6. Fascism (no political freedom; civil and economic freedom, and freedom of movement)
7. Dictatorship (minor political freedom; civil and economic freedom, and freedom of movement)
8. Socialism (controlled political and civil freedom; freedom of movement; government supervised economic freedom)
9. Plutocracy/Monarchy (supervised political freedom; civil and economic freedom, and freedom of movement)
10. Democracy (political, civil, and economic freedom, and freedom of movement)

Are you surprised that communism ranks third, better only for an incarcerated person or a slave? Are you surprised that Nazism is fifth and not worse than communism? This is because, even under Nazism or a theocracy, an individual (of the right race or religion) has more freedom than in communism. Regarding race, communism eliminates minorities and Jews as well, though not on the scale Hitler had perpetrated. And under communism religion is curtailed or forbidden. Unlike the Nazi, the ultimate killer of certain races, the communists are equal opportunity killers, if they don't find a use for you or you are against them.

Communism should not be confused with socialism. Former communist countries such as Romania called themselves Socialist Republics, but they were not socialist. The Western European democracies are socialist-inclined, but as long as there are free elections true socialist states take hold only temporarily. Free elections always corrects the imbalance between the working, tax paying people, and the ones that are taking advantage of the system.

Although democracy was abolished in communist Romania, occasional "for show" elections were held. However, you voted for one communist candidate per political seat. Why bother voting? Because it was quasi-mandatory, and the communists wanted to show that the selected candidates won with a majority of 99.9% support. I wonder who the 0.1% dissenters were?

All along I've pounded on communism and communists, for which I do not hide my dislike. The miserable life that communism brings to a country is not necessarily economic, but psychological. As a young man under communism, I felt tormented by an oppressive and dishonest totalitarian regime. I was only seventeen, and I couldn't stand it anymore. I was not in charge of my life, but the communist government was. I could make only limited decisions for myself. In communism you're allowed to do only what's permitted. Imagine trying to be of a free mind, trying to think outside the box, trying to invent something new without approval, trying to express yourself without fear of retaliation. You could do it, if you didn't value your life.

The communists tried to control everyone's thoughts, and in many cases they were very successful. It was like living in George Orwell's *1984*. I did not know the book, as it was banned in communist Romania, but when I read it I couldn't believe the similarities that I had experienced in communism with what the book described. Every day, through every channel of the media, the people were constantly told what a wonderful life they had, all because of the communist party. There were no rich to exploit the workers. The communist party abolished poverty and worked tirelessly for the betterment of the people. The reality was miserable.

Old Romanians knew how life had been in Romania before communism. The facts they related were at odds with what the communists were saying. The communists couldn't silence all the old Romanians who remembered, but what the communists could do and did was to rewrite the history, which was taught to the new generations. The new generations, including me, had no other knowledge except what we learned from school. The past was erased or changed to show everything from the point of view of communism. Every common thief and every terrorist of the past became heroes under communism, while the true national heroes were ignored or erased from history.

There was a problem, as I described in my story: The West was prospering under capitalism, and the material goods and occasional movies leaking into Romania were contradicting what the communists were telling us. The movies were labeled "capitalist propaganda," portraying life in the West as prosperous instead of showing the reality of people living in squalor, the unemployed, and workers on constant strike demanding better pay. What we weren't told was that the unemployed were compensated and the workers on strike, when working, earned 100 times more than the same worker in communist Romania, and none of them had to stand in line for food.

Why communism will fail:

- It is a one-party, absolutist political system, and no dissent is allowed.
- The party is ruled by an oligarchy.
- The worst psychopaths rise to power and become dictators.
- Communism cannot be voted out.
- Only communism's point of view and propaganda are allowed.
- A citizen must think and behave as the communist party decrees.
- It is a police state. The police protect the state from the people.
- Communism replaces God. It is an atheist culture.
- Dissenters are imprisoned or killed.
- All creative work is subject to censorship.
- All private properties from which profits could be made are owned by the state.
- All patented inventions and copyrights are owned by the state.
- All citizens become employees.
- Individual initiative is a liability.
- Mediocrity replaces meritocracy.
- Responsibility and accountability vanish.
- Inefficiency and poor quality plague the economy.
- National productivity diminishes.

- Scarcities of all goods become endemic.
- People's standard of living declines.
- Nepotism rules.
- Bribes are a way of life.
- Life expectancy decreases.
- The entire socio-economic culture declines and eventually collapses.

Communism is like a cancer. Once it takes hold of an organism, it doesn't let go until it kills it. The longer it holds power in a country the worse it will get, until communism either implodes or is eliminated through bloodshed.

The tragedy is that until communism runs its course and dies, millions of people will suffer and die at the hands of this monstrous political system.

BOOK 3. THE UNITED STATES OF AMERICA

"Thank you for freedom, America."

The United States of America is the number one country in the world, as far as I am concerned. I am privileged to live in this great country. I achieved more than I could have achieved anywhere else. Freedom is the best ingredient any nation needs in order to become prosperous. Thank God that the United States was powerful and stood up against communist expansionism and, in due course, precipitated its collapse. The United States is proof that when citizens have freedom, anything is possible. Try to control people's daily lives through government regulations, decrees, and police, and that country will shrivel.

The United States is evolving along with the rest of the world. It had and will have its ups and downs. Although the US was never in peril of being overrun by communism or the Soviet Union, the US had to be vigilant, and in the end it won the Cold War. At one time in the 1980s, the US was declared a stagnant economy, and Japan was about to overtake it. Instead, the US prospered and started the information technology revolution. Today, all eyes are on China. It is communist, but with a market economy, and, because of its low labor costs, most manufacturing moved there. Now China is about to overtake the United States as the biggest economy in the world. I bet my money on the USA; freedom is more powerful than communism, even in its current state in China.

I am proud to be an American citizen and pledge my allegiance to the United States of America. I pay taxes, I vote, and I have my own opinions about what's going on in this country. Of course, my opinions are filtered by the fact that I lived for my first eighteen years under a totalitarian regime, for which I hold no respect. For what I have written so far in this book, I would have been executed or imprisoned for life in the former communist Romania. Thank God for freedom, the US Constitution, and the first amendment.

1. POLITICIANS AND DEMOCRACY

"Politicians are the caste who buys votes from people with nothing to lose, with money taken from people with everything to lose."

Democracy is the best political system man has devised, although not perfect. Most of the electorate cast their votes with their feelings rather than with reason and logic. Sometimes the inept but well-liked wins over the competent but not-so-liked. Democracy is the most difficult political system to maintain. It can slide to the left into socialism and further down into the black hole of communism. Or it can slide to the right into fascism or theocracy.

In my opinion, our country has a bipolar democracy. We have a coexistence of socialist and plutocratic democracy. Why do I say the US is socialist? There are a few tests that, when applied, will tell us if the US is a socialist state:

1-You do not have to work to survive.

2-Less and less people pay taxes.

3-Prosperity declines.

4-The national debt increases, to pay for 1 & 2.

The USA did not become socialist through the hard work of communist academia or through the dogged determination of liberal media to change for the sake of change, or through the misguided beliefs of neo-communists in Hollywood. We got here because of our politicians. Yes, our elected officials, be those of the right or the left.

Politicians need money, lots of money, in order to be elected and re-elected. The plutocracy is their sponsors (plutocracy means the rich people, but when an entity, a special interest group, or a union has as much money as the rich, it belongs to the same category.) For a politician, no money means no chance of running for a political office. Politicians fall all over each other to please the rich and the special interest groups to obtain their money. The plutocracy will not contribute to a candidate because of ideological reasons; they contribute so they can influence the candidate to pass or maintain laws that favor them. *There's no free lunch, folks.* The money spent by the plutocracy is to even out the many votes of the have-nots against the few votes of the haves.

During an election campaign, a politician's job is to convince as many people as possible to vote for him or her. The majority of votes come from the middle class. The poor vote occasionally, and the rich are too few to make a difference when it comes to votes. Depending on the sentiment of the electorate, the politicians will tailor their speeches to resonate with the mood du jour.

Regardless of what politicians will say to get elected, all politicians are in competition with each other during elections. Competition is good for the consumers when it comes to commerce, and it is good for the electorate when it comes to politics. The people who have to compete, like politicians, hate competition. The Holy Grail for a politician is to be elected and re-elected without effort or opposition.

189

The politicians have figured out how to play the game in their favor and assure themselves of as large and faithful an electoral bloc as possible. They do it by granting favors to the electorate with our tax money. After they're elected, politicians grant legal favors to their sponsors, the plutocracy, and to their captive and faithful electorate with social programs. The middle class gets empty promises.

The plutocracy gets government contracts, laws that protect industries, laws that maintain the status quo and therefore prevent new competition, and, most importantly, tax breaks. Our tax codes are so complex and riddled with loopholes that they would make the old Byzantium seem a fair and honest place to do business.

The captive and needy voters get rewarded as well, by having their entitlements maintained and expanded. Have you wondered why the most financially distressed municipalities in the US always vote for the same party, in this case, the Democratic Party? What are the Democrats promising to that electorate, but more of the same: "Don't worry, be happy." What would the Republicans bring to the table? Pain and suffering, because that's what it will take to fix a financially blighted community. Do more and receive less is required. Who wants to vote for pain and suffering? Not many, even if it means their status in the long run will improve.

Needy voters will always vote for the candidate who promises more financial help. Now let's be honest: We don't want the needy to line our streets and beg for food and shelter. A wealthy country should provide for the needy. Even the staunchest conservative would be hard-pressed to say otherwise. However, there is a difference between the truly needy, the ones who are mentally or physically handicapped and cannot work to provide for themselves, and the politically transformed needy. Many of us have been transformed into the needy recently.

I heard a funny story once: This guy decided to give a few crackers to a raccoon visiting his backyard. The raccoon was so cute. The next evening, there were two raccoons, so he fed them both. They were so cute. The third night, there were four of them. He fed them because they, too, were cute. By the end of the week there was an entire clan of raccoons coming over for dinner. He ran out of crackers and decided to stop feeding them. Do you think the raccoons went foraging elsewhere? No. Food was too easy to obtain at this guy's house, and they gathered for several days at his back door, begging for food. Some even scratched at the door, demanding their daily meal. Eventually they got the message and found food the old way.

Why scavenge through trashcans like raccoons when food, good food, is provided for free and without effort? If you go to any national park, you'll see signs that read, "Don't feed the animals." One reason is that our human food may not be good for wild animals. But the worst part is that the animals get used to obtaining food without much effort, and they forget how to forage for themselves. When temperatures descend, people stop coming. The animals wonder where the effortless food is. Unless they remember how they used to nourish themselves before, they will have a hard time surviving.

And so will humans. Able people are converted into needy ones under the guise of the greater society. In reality, they become locked-in voters, so the politicians will get re-elected.

Today, there are a lot of negative feelings among people about our politicians, and for good reason. Politicians do little but talk in addressing our problems, like our national deficit. But why should they? Maintaining the status quo is safe, at least for the moment. As they say, delay and pray. Taking action is risky, mistakes could be made, and some or all politicians could lose their jobs.

Running for political office is supposed to be a civic duty. Our Founding Fathers did it that way. Today, being a politician is a profession, providing a very good job, perks, and prestige. No politician wants to lose such juicy employment. What will they do if they don't get re-elected? Get a real job, like the rest of us? That will be such a hardship.

The successful politicians have mastered the art of election and re-election. Studies show that over 95% of incumbents get re-elected in stable economic times. Therefore, with such a high rate of established professional politicians in power, who know everyone, know every trick, and pass laws that ensure that the electorate become captive voters, do we have a true democracy anymore?

Would a professional politician who lives the good life "serving" the people be able to relate to the common man and woman struggling to survive? I think not. And if we have elected politicians who are lifers and aloof from what real life is, doesn't this system resemble a totalitarian political system? That may seem like a stretch to call our politicians totalitarians. But if you and I cannot vote them out of power, what do we have but a bunch of insiders who maintain the status quo for their own advantage, voting their own pay raises and special medical and retirement plans that the rest of us could only dream of.

Luckily, we managed to limit the president's position to two terms. That prevents our country from having dictator-presidents. If Nixon hadn't gotten into trouble with Watergate, he could have been a good candidate for dictator. Today, Bill Clinton could have been our president since 1992, twenty years in power and running for another term in 2012.

In my opinion, we need to limit all elected positions to so many terms, say three terms for the House of Representatives and one term for the Senate, and no more than twelve years in

Congress, combined. Once politicians have served their civic duty, they should return to their private lives and make a living like the rest of us. Democracy doesn't mean the people get to elect the politicians, but the politicians need to be recycled as often as possible. Longevity in politics does not produce progress, only institutional sclerosis.

In the end, every country has the political system it deserves. We, the voters in the United States, by agreeing or disagreeing, have voted into power a quasi-totalitarian-socialist-plutocratic democracy.

2. ENTITLEMENTS

"Vote for me and the government will provide for you."

The largest financial giveaways are our entitlements, Social Security and Medicare. When Social Security was first instituted, it was painless, like all socialist programs are in the beginning. A very small amount was required from many to pay for a few of the elderly to eliminate poverty in old age. It was a good thing, since people behave mostly like the grasshopper and not like the ant. The problem with Social Security (and all other tax-paid social programs) is that it is a pyramid scheme: rob Peter to pay Paul. Today's workers pay for today's retirees. What happens when the workers equal the retirees? The whole system collapses.

I am approaching the time when I will be able to collect Social Security benefits. As of 2012, I paid into Social Security for forty years. In these years I contributed more to Social Security than to my 401k. But that money paid for past retirees. When I get to receive my benefits, will I vote for the candidate who wants to reduce my benefits? Not a chance. I, too, became a needy voter, a captive voter for the candidate who will maintain my life style, and that's what socialism is.

Young people are idealists. They want to transform mankind into a better world, and they usually are inclined to vote for socialist candidates. Youth and idealism create a paradox when it comes to social entitlements. Taxpayers, working people, pay for social programs, not the rich people. The votes young people cast today for socialist programs are the taxation noose that they will have around their necks tomorrow. Without realizing it, voting for what seems to be humane and fair is the price they'll pay in the future. When the young people of today are overburdened by the taxes of tomorrow, they will only have to blame their past voting habits.

Social Security, Medicare, welfare, food stamps, and other social benefits are examples of socialism. If you disagree that the US has become a socialist country, think of what portion of the US budget is consumed by Social Security, Medicare, and all other entitlements. It is at least 55%. And what happens when the government cannot collect enough taxes to pay for social programs and other obligations? It borrows.

OK, so what should FDR have done, instead of initiating a socialist Social Security program? I believe that all societies should take care of the elderly and sick, but not in a socialist way, in a capitalist way. Let's be honest, not every person thinks and saves for the rainy days. Socialism provides a safety net for the needy paid by the taxpayers. Capitalism provides a safety net paid through self-funding by each individual. The government should mandate that we all save a percentage of our wages for our retirement. How dare they force us to save? It is for our own good. And the money saved is our personal money. If all my Social Security deductions had been placed in my own personal retirement account and earned Treasury securities' interest rates, I would have over a million dollars today. I personally don't have anything near that amount in my 401k. The money saved under a mandatory retirement program couldn't be touched until retirement age, and then only as an annuity with rights of inheritance.

How about Medicaid and Medicare? Unfortunately, most of us don't think about saving for medical needs until we have a medical need. In the US, until recently with ObamaCare, we did not have national socialized medicine, except for the retired people who paid into Medicare. Instead, we have corporate social medicine. We rely on our employers to buy health insurance for us. The problem is that if you are unemployed you have no health insurance. We think that health insurance obtained through our jobs is free. It is not. We, all of us, pay for it. It is built into the prices we pay for goods and services.

Since we already pay for our health costs anyway, why not have capitalist health insurance? From birth, give every person a medical voucher of a certain amount. The money is to be spent on medical needs and is non-transferable. The amount on the voucher, if not used, is accumulated in a personal account that earns interest. In your younger years the money may not be needed, but with compound interest, the medical nest egg will grow by the time you get older.

This voucher amount could not provide for a liver or heart transplant, and additional health insurance will be needed for major medical needs. But at least the vouchers will provide for general medical care at a low cost to taxpayers, while relieving corporations from having to carry medical costs. (Corporations pass the cost of health insurance, just like the taxes they pay, to consumers anyway.)

The voucher system should be kept in a trust, away from the politicians, who would spend our money the way they did our Social Security funds.

Additionally, when you pay out of your own pocket through a voucher, you'll be a lot more judicious on how the money is spent. The whole system will become more efficient when every individual is responsible for his or her own retirement and health care. It will make every citizen independent of the government. But it will also require each one of us to think. Politicians know that thinking for ourselves is tough, so they give us the social safety net, the easy way. Don't worry, be happy, vote for me, and the government will provide for you. As long as we are in debt to the politicians for our survival they will continue to be re-elected while we slowly sink.

Socialism is based on transferring wealth from people who work and pay taxes to people who don't. Corporate taxation doesn't apply, because taxes for corporations are the cost of doing business. Taxes are added to product prices, and consumers eventually pay for them. It is the individual that is at the end of the line, the ultimate taxpayer. As long as there are many taxpayers versus social programs recipients, the socialist system works.

To paraphrase Margaret Thatcher, "Socialism is wonderful as long as you don't run out of other people's money." (That is, taxpayers and borrowed money.) The moment when the number of social-program recipients equals the number of taxpayers, the socialist system will be in jeopardy. The politicians will sustain the system by borrowing in the hope that more taxes may be collected at a later time. When that doesn't happen, the socialist state will collapse.

It will be very painful to switch from a socialist system to a capitalist one. When that happens, we will have two choices: rebuild the system the right way or fall into communism.

3. TAXES AND CORPORATE WELFARE

"Simple is easily attacked, complicated is easily defended."

One of the easiest ways for politicians to confuse us is to make a simple concept complicated. Such a concept is taxation. The more complicated taxation becomes, the more "spin" a politician can put on that subject, such as:

The rich don't pay their fair share.

or

If the rich pay more taxes, there will be less investment and job creation.

The more complicated the tax code is, the more loopholes and breaks the politicians can give to their sponsors.

Taxes can be simple: one rate for all. All right, several rates so the rich will pay more and prevent them for getting even richer. Why would the average employed earner in this country have to become a bean counter, or hire one to do their income taxes in April? Leave that for businesses. But no, the more complicated the issue, the more snow jobs we get from the politicians, and we don't dare ask for simple taxes.

Until now, I have talked about the money a socialist system is spending on the needy or newly converted needy. The government spends huge amounts on corporations, which are

198

"justified" for job creation. And that's fine, I guess, until we talk about the financial disaster of 2008, when our taxes were spent on corporate welfare, because those institutions were too big to fail. There is a reason why we have antitrust laws, to prevent any business enterprise from dominating and setting its will on the economy. What is *too big to fail* but another term for monopoly?

Unfortunately, nothing was fixed after the 2008 financial disaster. Instead, we have now even bigger institutions that cannot fail. Capitalism rewards the good businesses and punishes the bad ones. Now the bad businesses can continue to be bad, and we, the taxpayers, compensate for their losses. Communism would not let any business fail. There is no difference between communism and what our elected officials did after 2008. Without exception, those financial institutions that ruined many of us are profitable now and continue the same risky business as before.

Between the money borrowed to sustain the social programs and corporate welfare, the US and state governments have accumulated substantial debt. The debt can be paid from additional taxes, which means that you and I pay them. Or we can allow inflation, which will diminish the value of the debt. Again, you and I are the losers when prices go up but our income stays put. The US could devalue the dollar and lower our purchasing power, which could be similar to inflation. Or the US could default on the debt. Unthinkable? When you run out of money and places to borrow more money, everything is possible.

4. WEALTH

Where there are no rich people, there is no prosperity.

The United States and its people used to be very wealthy. We still are wealthy, but not so much after the financial disaster of 2008. Wealth brings stability to any country, and it has provided a great deal of stability to our country. Democracy is always most stable when there is a large middle class. But after 2008, a lot of the middle class became poorer.

Although the Great Recession of 2008 was caused by the collapse of real estate values and the misdoings of financial institutions and Wall Street, the recovery was slow, and it will continue to be slow because the entire makeup of the United States economy has changed.

About twenty years ago, I was listening to a financial and investment radio station. I heard a very interesting point of view from one of the commentators. He said, "Wealth is accumulated in two ways: by creation or by transfer." In other words, an individual, or a country for that matter, can become wealthy by creating wealth or transferring wealth, or a combination of create and transfer, which is what really happens.

Wealth creation always makes use of the 5 Ms (Mind-Money-Machine-Material-Men.) For wealth transfer, however, the five elements don't have to be present; mostly absent are the Machine and/or the Material. (Computers could be considered machines, but investments and financial calculations were made without computers in the past, so they shouldn't count as machines.)

Farmers plant seeds on their land and create wealth. Mining companies extract ore out of the ground and create wealth. Manufacturers use raw materials, produce goods, and create wealth. Builders build houses and infrastructures and create wealth. In short, agriculture, mining, construction, and any other industry creates wealth.

Financial and banking institutions transfer wealth. Wall Street transfers wealth, and so do the insurance companies. Lawsuits are transfers of wealth. Any services, from taxi drivers and dry cleaners to restaurants, doctors, and nursing care, are transfers of wealth.

Transferring wealth is not bad in and of itself. If it weren't for doctors, we wouldn't be living this long. If it weren't for financial institutions, we would be trading seashells for goods. And if it weren't for Wall Street providing the capital, enterprises wouldn't start. Even lawsuits are a kind of policing to punish wrongdoers. The transfer of wealth is a sign of how rich a country is. But if there's too much transferring and no creating, soon there will be little to transfer. If a country has no wealth, there is nothing to transfer.

The ultimate transferor of wealth is the government. Taxation is wealth transfer. For sure, a lot of this wealth is put to good uses, such as education, infrastructure, the military and police to keep us safe, and laws to protect our rights and make commerce easier. And there is the transfer of wealth for social programs, 55% of the budget and climbing, just like the interest we pay for the national debt.

There is no major country that can thrive without some wealth creation, although there can be some smaller countries that can do quite well by transferring wealth. In this case I'm referring to tourism or banking and financial services.

The United States economy in 2011 consisted of 23% from the agricultural and industrial sectors and 77% from the service sector. In other words, wealth creation was 23% and wealth transfer, 77%. This is not bad, considering that 23% of our economy creates enough wealth to support the other 77% in wealth transferring. However, the less wealth creation our economy will have, the less prosperity for all. In the recent past we all have heard about manufacturing moving to China. Manufacturing is wealth creation. Those high-paying jobs leave the US and move to another country. The United States cannot survive on tourism and agriculture alone.

The 2008 recession has eliminated a large number of wealth creation jobs, because the enterprises employing those workers were uncompetitive. Once bankrupt, those businesses could not re-build. And those jobs are gone forever. They will not return, even if the economy improves, because as long as China is the cheap labor country, our wealth creation jobs will be there, and we will have less wealth to transfer among ourselves.

Wealth transfer caused the events culminating in the 2008 recession. The financial institutions created the real estate bubble, from which they profited at the expense of the middle class. Our government covered whatever losses the banks may have had. It must be good to be a banker to profit when the economy is booming and when the economy is in recession. And for the rest of us who lost our houses in foreclosure, we lost them because of wealth transfer getting out of control.

When I came to the United States in 1972, I was surprised that the rich were not hated, as I was told they were when I grew up in communism. The rich were admired and inspirational to the many people who aspired to become rich. Individual initiative, smarts, and hard work allowed people to become rich and, in turn, they made the nation rich. With that kind of attitude among the people, freedom, and a government that encouraged wealth

202

building and accumulation, the USA is the most powerful economy in the world.

Building toward 2008 and after, "rich" became a dirty word. For sure, the rich financiers and Wall Street speculators are the major villains in the economic catastrophe culminating in 2008. They haven't done much to dispel that sentiment and continue their financial-pyramid-scheme building with impunity and with the help of our politicians. As long as a few greedy rich people continue their quest to enrich themselves through wealth transfer to the detriment of everyone else, the well-being of our economy will continue to decline.

The sentiments of the population have tilted toward favoring the government to save us from our financial distress. The Democratic Party in essence has become a socialist party nowadays, and many people are lured into believing that the government, not individual effort, is the key to prosperity. Where there are no rich people, there is no prosperity. Bad as that may sound, it is the cold, sober truth.

I was dismayed when Mitt Romney was attacked for being rich, for earning his wealth through smarts and hard work. As long as we believe that the rich are the problem, and the politicians and bureaucrats are the answer, the more we will decline in our prosperity. The money the government has to give away comes from the working people, including the rich. The government never creates any wealth, and without wealth creation we are doomed.

Our economic situation has a major influence on our political situation. However, the wealthier our nation becomes, the more revenue our state and federal governments have, the more money will be spent on frivolous or socialist causes. The poorer our nation becomes, the more need there will be to spend money on social benefits, and the more we will borrow to help ourselves. For the foreseeable future, the United States will continue to slide to the left into socialism, and the middle class will shrink.

5. THE FUTURE

"Any prediction of the future, if enough people believe in it, will become reality."

What's in store for America? Will it continue on the path of decline, or re-emerge as prosperous again? Will it continue sliding into socialism or keep in the center of the political spectrum?

Economically, the US will be number one in the world. However, it will continue to be prosperous only through innovation and freedom from regulations and overtaxation. There will be two classes of people: the prosperous ones working on the leading edge of American innovation, and the ones who will work in globally competitive jobs that will not pay as well.

There will be two things that will improve the life of US workers competing with the rest of the world's workers: the cost of energy and automation. If the cost of energy soars, it will be unprofitable to move products overseas from China to the US, and manufacturing jobs will relocate here. If automation will achieve a robotic level of sophistication such that labor costs will become less significant, then manufacturing jobs will relocate back here. However, the robotic jobs will be fewer and highly skilled. Education is the key.

Politically, the US has a perilous road ahead. The more prosperous the population will be, the more we will stay in the center of the political spectrum. The greater the decline in the standard of living, the more socialist we will become. Socialism will consume all the stored wealth of the country until the US will collapse economically.

Our constitutional rights are under constant challenge. With the terrorist threats, Homeland Security has infringed on those rights and, lately, with the infamous video and Benghazi killings, the first amendment seems to be threatened. Nowadays you almost have to self-censor and not disseminate material that may be deemed offensive by our government and foreigners. The producer of the infamous video was all but assured to end up in jail, especially when a technicality was ready at hand to arrest him. The US government condemned the video and explicitly condemned our first amendment as if we were a banana republic that offended a great power and our civil liberties were a crime.

Upon the collapse of the US, the communists will be on hand to take over. However, there is a large silent majority that is fed up pressing 1 for English, making us a United Nations instead of the United States; fed up being told that we are not a Christian nation and that our government is atheist; and fed up seeing our jobs going to China, paying more and more in taxes, and seeing our wealth eroded by inflation. The backlash against communism will be fascism.

In times of crisis, democracy doesn't work, and radical elements of the political spectrum will take over. There will be a struggle between communism and fascism. The United States is not the Russia of 1917. It will resemble the Germany of the 1920s. Remember how Hitler came to power? The American population is an armed society, and it will not be cowered into communism. Unfortunately, we may turn fascist.

I hope prosperity will return and flourish, and that democracy and freedom will survive for us, our children, and our grandchildren.

The End

If you enjoyed this book and would like to help other readers with your comments please write a review on Amazon, which I appreciate very much. Amazon books link.

For more information about my books and my art please visit my website: sandru.com

For your reading delight I included the first chapter from "Hitler Was a Socialist" that will give you a better understanding of Communism-Socialism.

Read this book and find out what the Marxists-Socialists are afraid of.

THIS BOOK IS PROHIBITED FOR ADVERTISEMENT ON AMAZON

Chapter 1. Hitler Was a Socialist?

WTF? Adolf Hitler was a Socialist? Preposterous! Blasphemy against the International Socialist Cause! Who would say a thing like that?

As noted in "Adolf Hitler" by John Toland, Adolf Hitler in 1927, at Clou restaurant center in Berlin said:

> **We are socialists, we are enemies of today's capitalistic economic system for the exploitation of the economically weak, with its unfair salaries, with its unseemly evaluation of a human being according to wealth and property instead of responsibility and**

performance, and we are determined to destroy this system under all conditions. [16: pg. 224-225]

Does this sound like fascism to you? Or maybe something like comrade Lenin, or campanero Castro, or, shall I dare say, socialist Bernie Sanders would say? But Hitler said it. In his own words he considered himself a socialist and anti-capitalist just like Marxism-Socialism advocates.

The above speech from Hitler is erroneously assigned to Gregor Strasser. Per the book "Hitler" by Joachim Fest, Hitler's speech was afterwards published in the Nazi Paper *Völkischer Beobachter* whose editor was Gregor Strasser, and therefore attributed to Gregor Strasser. The Marxist professors have gone out of their way to separate Hitler's National-Socialism from Marxist-Socialism. Some information on the Internet cannot be trusted due to zealous efforts of the Marxists to change the history per their ideology, as they always do, Hitler including.

However, what's more important to understand is what Hitler and the NAZI-Socialists did. This book will be an eye opener for anyone who's of the opinion that he was a fascist. Instead Hitler was a first class Socialist.

I realize that many people are sickened of learning what Hitler did, and others prohibit knowing anything about him, however, I found out that unlike the Marxists-Socialists who hide behind slogans while enslave nations, and kill anyone opposing them, Hitler was straight forward about what he did, how he did it, and why he undertook his National-Socialism revolution. Yes, his coming to power was a bloodless revolution, a Socialist revolution, and for that he is feared by the Marxist-Socialists.

National-Socialism is the opponent to Marxism-Leninism-Communism-Socialism. If we don't learn from history, it is bound to repeat again in the future.

Fasten your seatbelts, folks, and learn who Hitler and the NAZI-Socialist party really were. By analyzing side by side Marxism-Socialism and National-Socialism you will see that they are identical, except for one point, which is misunderstood. Adolf Hitler was a monster and that will never change. But he was a *socialist* monster like the rest of them.

In another of his speeches Hitler said:

> The world is not here for a few people, and an order based eternally on the distinction between the haves and the have-nots does not exist anymore because the have-nots have determined to lay claim to their portion of God's earth. [4: Munich - April 12, 1922]

Hitler is allying with the have-nots to lay claim to their portion of earth. Fascists exploit the have-nots; they do not share the God's Earth with them. Only a Socialist would definitely do that.

The following is an extract from an interview with Adolf Hitler by George Sylvester Viereck, which took place in 1923, answering the question about socialism. It was republished in *Liberty* magazine in July 1932, and it appeared in *theguardian.com*:

"Why," I asked Hitler, "do you call yourself a National Socialist, since your party programme is the very antithesis of that commonly accredited to socialism?"

"Socialism," he retorted, putting down his cup of tea, pugnaciously, "is the science of dealing with the common weal. Communism is not Socialism. Marxism is not Socialism. The Marxians have stolen the term and confused its meaning. I shall take Socialism away from the Socialists.

"Socialism is an ancient Aryan, Germanic institution. Marxism has no right to disguise itself as socialism. Socialism, unlike Marxism, does not repudiate private property. Unlike Marxism, it involves no negation of personality, and unlike Marxism, it is patriotic.

"We chose to call ourselves the National Socialists. We are not internationalists. Our socialism is national." [14]

The interviewer was of the opinion that Marxism meant socialism, but Hitler considered true socialism his version of National-Socialism, and he definitely didn't want to be confused with Marxism. The world Marxist cause thinks Marxism is the only Socialist cause. In reality they both are socialist causes.

We were told that Adolf Hitler and the NAZIs were Fascist. And who told us that? Joseph Stalin, the mass murderer of the USSR. Why? It is on account of Benito Mussolini and his Italian

Fascist Party, which successfully came to power in Italy, and in spite of the name, *Fascist*, the party was a Socialist party as well. Not all Socialist parties were Marxist-Leninist, and those other socialist parties Vladimir Ilych Lenin considered non-socialist because they were not controlled by Moscow. Therefore, in 1928 Joseph Stalin issued the order that only the Marxist-Leninist parties were *Socialists*, and everyone else was *Fascist*, as Mussolini's Fascist party was named.

And we *obeyed*.

Hitler's party was the NAZI party, or in German, NSDAP, National*sozialistische* Deutsche Arbeiterpartei. In English, NAZI means the National *Socialist* German *Workers'* Party. As a matter of fact, Hitler never called himself a fascist, but a *Nationalsozialistische*, a *National Socialist*. Yes, Hitler and the Nazis may have allied themselves with the likes of Italy's Fascist Mussolini and Spain's Falangist Franco governments, but Hitler and the NAZIs were not a fascist party, nor did they consider themselves fascists; just as the alliance between the United States and the Soviet Union during WW II did not make the United States a communist-socialist country.

OK, just because the words *Socialist* and *Workers* were included in the party's name that doesn't make NAZI or Hitler *Socialist*.

Maybe we need to understand what *Socialism* or *Socialist* really means.

Socialism can come in more convictions than Marxist-Socialism and Communist-Socialism. It can be Democratic-

Socialism, Christian-Socialism, even feudal-socialism, agricultural-socialism, and bourgeois-socialism of the nineteenth century. In the evolution from feudalism into a new social order, the word *socialism* was used to represent the masses, the society's rise to power.

According to F. Engels, [1] *The Communist Manifesto* was not called *The Socialist Manifesto* because in 1847 Socialism signified the bourgeois and other movements, whereas Communism signified working-class movements. But since then, all socialist movements have been identified mistakenly as Marxism-Socialism, and since the collapse of the communist economic systems and the discrediting of Communism, the leftists have renamed themselves as Socialists, Marxists, Leftists, Liberals, or Progressives.

Socialism is the same horror house under a new name and management.

The socialism known today is based on *The Communist Manifesto* by Karl Marx and Friedrich Engels, published in 1848, which was a turbulent revolutionary year.

Regardless of what type of *socialism* we discuss, all types of socialism have one thing in common: They try to benefit their society through a unified dogma applicable to all members without any deviation or reinterpretation, meaning that society's rule is imposed on all individuals of that society with no exception. Individual freedom is subservient to the common cause of socialism or the community.

Communism is guided by Marxist-Leninist rules, and at its core is the immutable principle that the state in the name of society owns all the wealth of the nation for the common good of all, and *no individual* can enrich himself/herself from or profit through another man's work, asset, capital, mineral rights, land, inheritance, or anything that will make that individual *rich*, in other words, *not needing to work.*

The Marxist-Socialists object to calling Hitler a Socialist because he never confiscated the wealth of the rich. For pragmatic reasons, as you will see, Hitler chose to let the economy remain in the hands of the capitalists, and allow them to keep their assets and even prosper. It is true, Hitler did not confiscate the wealth of his nation's rich.

However,

he planned on confiscating other nation's wealth; that of the USSR.

All socialist regimes have an inherent inability to stay in power in a country unless they have dictatorial powers, and they will kill to maintain the absolute power they have to enforce their socialist principles.

From *How Socialist Was Adolf Hitler?*:

Professor Stackelberg also makes it plain in his work that he considers the Left to be the "progressive" end, and although he accepts that at the extreme ends of the spectrum there will be "movements who will go to any lengths to achieve their utopian ideal... [8]

213

Yes, be that the Marxist-Socialists, the Marxist-Leninists, or National-Socialists they will go to any lengths, including murdering hundreds of millions of people to achieve their socialist ideal.

Totalitarian Socialism of any kind—Communist-Socialist or National-Socialist—is, as you'll see, the biggest killer in human history.

Other Books by Dumitru (Mit, DG) Sandru

Non-Fiction, Political

Freedom Trumps Socialism: How the Democrat Party is Using Hitler's Playbook to Make America Socialist" by Dumitru Sandru.

THIS BOOK IS PROHIBITED FOR ADVERTISEMENT ON AMAZON

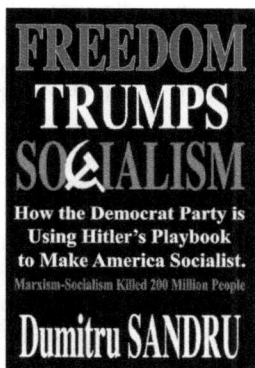

FREEDOM
TRUMPS
SOCIALISM
How the Democrat Party is
Using Hitler's Playbook
to Make America Socialist.
Marxism-Socialism Killed 200 Million People

Dumitru SANDRU

Do you fear expressing your political views? Why Socialism destroyed every country it governed? Why is Socialism appealing? How Socialist is the United States of America? How to prevent Socialism? Who is responsible for the upcoming demise of America? Who created the WOKE Zombies? What is the World Great Reset? What is Socialism, or Communism, and what the future holds for America? Why the Critical Race Theory is racist and demeaning to the black race? Why do they want the police defunded? Who are the Fascists in America? Why are the white men regarded as the Jews in Nazi-Germany? Why is Communist China a Fascist country? Who were and are the American Socialist Presidents? Should we pay reparations to the blacks? What are the BLM demands? Who is Antifa?

Hitler Was a Socialist, by Dumitru Sandru, A Comparison of NAZI-Socialism, Communism, Marxism-Socialism, and the United States

THIS BOOK IS PROHIBITED FOR ADVERTISEMENT ON AMAZON

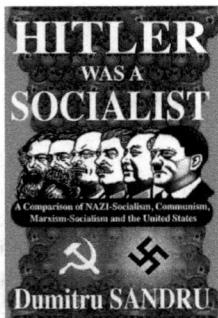

We associate Fascism with NAZI and Adolf Hitler. Wrong!

Adolf Hitler and the National Socialist Worker's Party, NAZI, was a Socialist party.

Then who told us that Hitler and the NAZI were Fascist? Joseph Stalin, the mass murderer of the USSR said so. And the rest of the world obeyed.

It is time to uncover the truth.

Adolf Hitler was a monster, a Socialist monster, as all Socialists are. The facts are out there in plain sight, but the Marxist Academia and media will not consider talking about the truth, least it would tarnish the "good" reputation of the Communism-Socialism, which killed 200 million people worldwide.

Socialism, we must fear, not fascism.

Escape from Communism, by Dumitru Sandru, a True Story and Commentary.

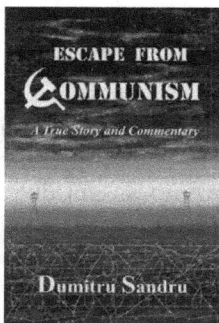

Life under communism is cruel and inhumane. Commit the smallest political infraction, and the secret police will arrest you. The only ray of hope is the West, but it is a crime to escape by crossing the border illegally, and anyone caught is beaten and imprisoned, sometimes even shot. This is my story of what happened and how I reached freedom.

Paranormal, Mystery, Thriller

The Pregnant Pope (Book 1 TIO Series), by Mit Sandru.

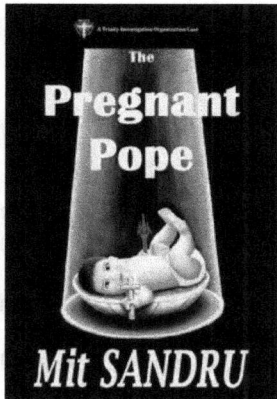

The 92-year-old Pope is pregnant. He hasn't undergone any medical procedures, but he carries a fetus in his abdomen. Is this a case of self-cloning, or a mutation? Is this an Immaculate Conception, or Satan's work? Find out how Claire, Travis, and Prescott solve this mystery and the bizarre outcome.

The Devolution of Adam and Eve (Book 2 TIO Series) by Mit Sandru

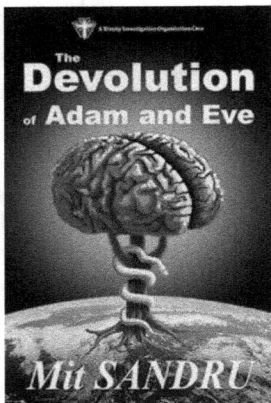

A pandemic causes billions of people to lose their minds. The world's government health agencies cannot identify the pathogen and develop an antidote. It comes from another realm, and only Claire, Prescott, and Travis can solve this enigma. Will they prevent the end of humanity before it's too late?

Teen, Children Fantasy

Arboregal, the Lorn Tree, by D.G. Sandru.

YouTube: **https://bit.ly/2OtDj5c**

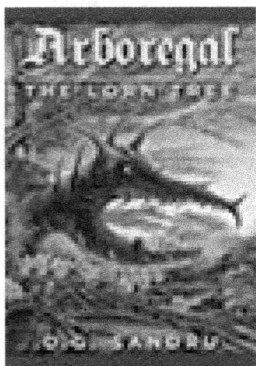

Four youngsters, Melissa, Perry, Nathan and Michelle materialize in a desolate world where giant, mile-high trees, support all life. They find shelter in the Lorn Tree among the Lorns. Soon after they discover that an evil spirit, Hellferata, wants them dead. Fearful Lorns want to expel the youngsters from their tree, which would be a dead sentence since monsters roam the land at night.

Will their ingenuity, cunning, and courage help them escape, or will

Hellferata mete out her wrath before they can escape?

Science Fiction

Sferogyls (Timurud Book 1) by Mit Sandru

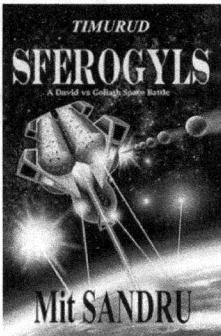

The Maggotroll Empire invades the Sferogyls' planet. The Sferogyls are unarmed and have no defense against the imperial battleships. The gods resurrect Timurud and send him to help the peaceful Sferogyls fight the invaders. Will the Sferogyls win the war in space and defend their planet, or perish?

Gold Rush Mystery (Terraspantion Chronicles, Bk. 1) by Mit Sandru.

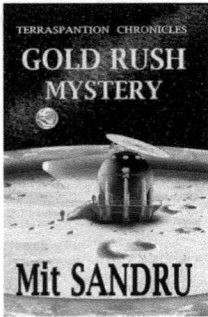

America is back on the Moon, and we intend to stay and establish a self-sustaining permanent base for tourism and mining. The work is challenging, the environment is deadly, but the astronauts Mia, Geo and Roby succeed in building the moon base, even if they landed in a mysterious crater.

Time Hole, (Terraspantion Chronicles, Bk. 2) by Mit Sandru.

Mining on the moon is a hazardous affair. Deedee and Arno, two lunar generalists, find perils beyond what they signed up for when they travel on the lunar surface at night . . . on the dark side of the Moon. Time will not be the same after they fall into the Time Hole.

Folding Reality, by Mit Sandru. Time Travel Adventure

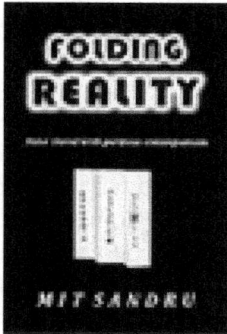

Mike the insurance salesman experiences perilous time travel experiences just by folding a piece of paper. He is crucified on Golgotha, almost gassed at Auschwitz, marooned in a Russian capsule going to the Moon.

Vampires - Thriller & Romance

YouTube: **https://bit.ly/2pahMDI**

YouTube: **https://bit.ly/2lPwAt4**

Vampire (Vlad V, Bk 1) by Mit Sandru.

Meeting a vampire isn't something that happens every night, even on the New York City subway. But never in her wildest dreams did Cat Sanders ever expect to meet the vampire Vlad V Draculesti and survive the encounter. Instead, she became his confidant. Why was she so lucky?

R.I.P., The Death of a Vampire (Vlad V, Bk 2) by Mit Sandru.

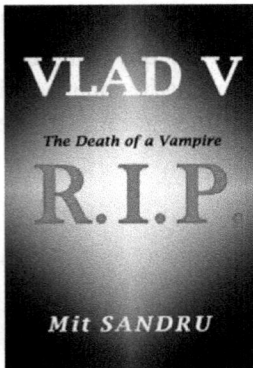

Vlad V Draculesti is dying because of an incident that happened decades ago. Unfortunately for Vlad V, the US intelligence agencies investigate him to find out his true identity, and centuries old life. Will Cat Sanders and vampire friends be able to help him die in peace, or will Vlad be discovered for being a vampire and die in a US Federal research laboratory?

Vampire Slayers (Vlad V, Bk 3) by Mit Sandru.

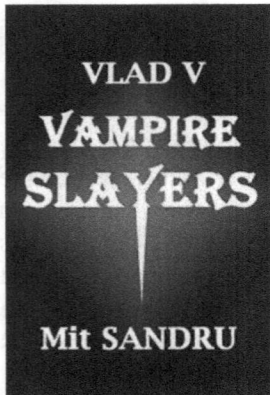

Cat Sanders is a billionaire, but not all is well. Her nemesis, Veronica Seyler, allied with a vampire-slayer drug cult, demands extortion money or she will be killed.

Cat's vampire friend, Angelique, comes to her aid. But the cult is more cunning and dangerous than even her vampire friend could handle. Would Cat and Angelique be able to come out of this alive even if Cat pays the ransom?

Vampires of Transylvania (Vlad V, Bk 4) by Mit Sandru

Cat Sanders has a simple task: spread Vlad V's ashes in Transylvania at midnight, during full moon. But in Transylvania Vlad V has centuries old enemies who take her and her friend Tudor hostage, placing them in iron cages among zombies and proto-vampires. Will they be able to escape from the blood sucking proto-vampires and flesh-eating zombies, or become zombies themselves?

The Queen of Vampires: A New Queen Arises (Vlad V, Bk 5) by Mit Sandru

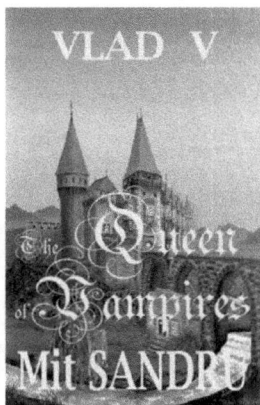

The Vampire Queen, Eleonore von Schwarzenberg, is bloodthirsty and vengeful on Cat Sanders and her friends. She plans the most painful death for them. Cat and her friends find themselves entrapped and helpless to avoid her wrath.

Will Cat and her friends be able to escape and survive the Queen of Vampires' fury?

Coloring Book

Abstract Dreams: Coloring Book 1 (Sandru's Art) by Dumitru Sandru

YouTube: **https://bit.ly/2Ulc9RT**

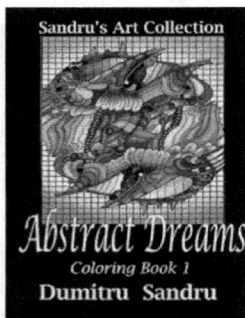

Reward your soul with the smooth and pleasing lines of Abstract Dreams

https://www.sandru.com/Coloring.html

Visit my e-Gallery at:

https://www.sandru.com/SferogylsArt.html

https://www.sandru.com/LornTreeArt.html

http://dumitru-sandru.artistwebsites.com/

https://www.pinterest.com/mitsandru/

T-Shirts and other stuff:

https://www.zazzle.com/store/dgsandru/products

About Dumitru "Mit" Sandru

Mit Sandru was born in the greater area of Transylvania in the last millennium; make that last century since he's not a vampire. Yet. When he was six years old, a soldier shot him at point blank range with a Kalashnikov. He survived. He outsmarted his German teacher, and survived a tornado in the middle of a wheat field. Not concurrently. When he was 18 years old, he escaped from a country resembling a concentration camp, luckily without being killed. He outran mean border patrol dogs in a foreign country, in the darkness of night, while jumping over six-foot tall stonewalls. Superman he's not. He came to the USA in search of freedom, glory, wealth, and fame. He's still searching for three of those. Lightning grazed him, and he caught a shark by the tail. Once. A monkey attacked him in Japan, but his daughter saved him. He avoided many rattlesnake bites, and built a house. No relation between the snakes and the house. Life eventually tamed him and he became a responsible citizen, with a wife, two daughters, dog and cat. And lately two grandsons. The taming part is questionable. He acquired an engineering and management degree and attempted to acquire other degrees in music, marketing, and IT. A certified student he is. He obtained many professional licenses, which he hardly used, but looked good on his wall. At 59-¾ years old he quit the corporate life and a six-figure salary. Rumor has it that he was given the golden handshake. He was finally free to pursue his dreams of writing, painting and music. During his professional life he painted hundreds of canvases, and composed dozens of tunes, while since his golden handshake he wrote 14 books; although one is a coloring book. And that was in just the first half of his life.

Disclaimer: Everything written here is true, but the bullets were blanks.

I am Mit Sandru and I approve this unabashed bio.

Want to see and read more about the second half of his life?

Webpage: http://sandru.com

Twitter: http://bit.ly/1kVzh6Z

Facebook: http://on.fb.me/1OiYOCn

Goodreads: http://bit.ly/1TgVbNa

Amazon: Amzn.to/1UtpTFR

Pinterest: https://www.pinterest.com/mitsandru/

YouTube videos

Arboregal, The Lorn Tree:

https://bit.ly/2OtDj5c

Abstract Dreams: Coloring Book 1:

https://bit.ly/2Ulc9RT

Vlad V Vampire Series:

https://bit.ly/2pahMDI

Lucy the Vampire Dog:

https://bit.ly/2lPwAt4

www.ingramcontent.com/pod-product-compliance
Lightning Source LLC
Chambersburg PA
CBHW072127270326
41931CB00010B/1692